Classroom Community Builders

Other Books by Alphabet Publishing

Successful Group Work
13 Activities to Teach Teamwork Skills
by Patrice Palmer

50 Activities for the First Day of School
Walton Burns

On the Board
200 Fast, Fun & Easy Warmer, Filler, and Fast-Finisher Activities
by Walton Burns

We are a small, independent publishing company that specializes in resources for teachers in the area of English language learning. We believe that a good teacher is resourceful, with a well-stocked toolkit full of ways to elicit, explain, guide, review, encourage and inspire. We help stock that teacher toolkit by providing teachers with books of practical and useful activities and techniques.

∽

Sign up for our mailing list on our website, www.alphabetpublishingbooks.com, to stay in touch, find out about our new books, and for deals and giveaways you won't find anywhere else.

Classroom Community Builders

Activities for the First Day & Beyond

WALTON BURNS

Classroom Community Builders
Activities for the First Day and Beyond
by Walton Burns

Copyright © 2017 Walton Burns

ISBN: 978-0-9977628-7-7 (paperback)
978-0-9977628-6-0 (ebook)

Library of Congress Control Number: 2017907358

All rights reserved. No part of this book may be reproduced, introduced into or stored in a retrieval system, or transmitted, in any form, or by any means (electronic, mechanical, photocopying, recording, or otherwise) without the prior written permission of the copyright holder.

Country of Manufacture Specified on the Last Page
First Printing 2017

Published by:
Alphabet Publishing
1204 Main Street #172
Branford, Connecticut 06405 USA

info@alphabetpublishingbooks.com
www.alphabetpublishingbooks.com

Contents

From the First Day to a Classroom Community	1

Set Your Expectations

Book Scan	6
Book Field Trip	8
Syllabus Scavenger Hunt	10
Sample Syllabus Scavenger Hunt	12
Classroom Rules Negotiation	13
What Does a Community Look Like?	15
My Favorite Teacher	16
Good Teacher / Good Student	17
Study Habit True and False	19
Language Learning Myths	20
What Do You Know?	23
Study Tip Share	24
Good Classroom Habit Role Play	25

Working Together

Different Thoughts	28
Sorting Line	30
In My Own Words	32
In My Own Words Poster	34
I am a Word	35
Sentence Auction	37
Cloze Paragraph	39
Sample Cloze Text	41
Don't Say It	43
Fill in the Picture	45
Sample Fill in the Picture	47
Picture Flashing	48

Sample Picture	50
Student Dictations	51
Sample Student Dictations	53
Twenty Questions	55
Culture Shock	57
Culture Shock Handout	59
Jigsaw Reading	60
Sample Jigsaw Reading	62
Classroom Scavenger Hunt	65
Simple Classroom Scavenger Hunt	67
Picture Words	68
Alibi	69
Follow the Directions	72
Follow the Directions Sample Task	74
Mystery Gap	76
The Break-In Mystery	77
Scenes from a Hat	79
Difficult Situation	81
A Difficult Situation Letter	82
Judgment	83
Collaborative Stories	84
Questions First	86
Reverse Story Picture	87
Sample Picture for Reverse Picture Telling	88
Plane Crash Survival	89
Plane Crash Survival Worksheet	91
Mission to Mars	93
Mission to Mars Worksheet	94
Settlements	95
Settlements Map	96
Create a New Country	97

Constitution for a New Country	98
Debate	100
Discussion Question	103
Pyramid Discussion	104
Role Play	106
Beauty, Inc. Role Play	109
Cultural Role Play	112
Cultural Role Play Cards	115

Getting to Know You Activities

Name Tents	118
Going on a Picnic Easy Version	119
Going on a Picnic Guessing Game	121
Toss a Ball	123
Fun Fact Memory Chain	125
Where Are You From?	127
Same and Different	128
Identity Circles	129
Me Bag	130
3-2-1 Introduction	132
3-2-1 Introduction Worksheet	134
Never Have I Ever, Classroom Edition	135
Who Wrote That?	137
Class Averages	138
Class Survey	139
Group Profile	140
4-3-2 Fluency Intro	142
Snowball Fight	144
Snowball "Texting"	145

Get to Know Your Teacher

First Day Letter	148

Ask the Teacher	150
Tell Me about Me	151
Correct the Teacher	152
Answers on the Board	153

Tips for Building Community   159

Considerations for Grouping Students   157

About the Author   160

Picture Credits   161

From the First Day to a Classroom Community

My first book with Alphabet Publishing was a collection of activities for the first day of class called, simply enough, *50 Activities for the First Day of School*. In it, I shared activities that helped students start working together from the first day. There were a number of name learning and icebreakers, as well as activities to start assessing and practicing language, and to set the tone and expectations of the classroom community. Generally, teachers seemed to like it.

However, while discussing the book, I was introduced to the debate about icebreakers and classroom community activities. For example, many teachers question whether icebreakers are an effective method of getting students to bond or a waste of time. Or can we design better icebreakers?

Perhaps putting students straight to work is the best way to build community. Some teachers even suggested that classroom community wasn't important to learning. As teachers, content should come first, the argument went. We don't have to like each other to study together, do we?

As I reflected on these perspectives, I looked at my own practice, read up on some of the research, and chatted with other teachers. I even wrote some articles here and there about the topic to try to get feedback from other teachers and writers[1].

Research and classroom experience do show that students do better in classrooms where they feel included and welcome. In fact, some research suggests that the biggest determiner of whether a group will be successful is how safe and supported the team members

---

1   For example: https://www.middleweb.com/32689/dont-break-the-ice-build-your-community/

feel[2]. Put simply, if a student doesn't feel they can speak freely in the classroom or make mistakes, that student won't participate fully in class. Spending time helping students get to know each other a bit and practicing teamwork skills is clearly time well spent.

On the other hand, it is true that teaching teamwork skills and doing icebreakers cuts into class time. I don't know of any teacher who feels that they have too much class time. Furthermore, students like to walk away from class feeling that they have accomplished something besides learning that Peng's favorite color is blue. So perhaps instead of empty icebreakers, we can look at teamwork activities that are also relevant to the content of the class. Rather than choosing between teaching our subject or doing community building activities, we can find activities that do both.

This book, which is a sort of second edition to *50 Activities for the First Day of School,* but also something of a new entity on its own, attempts to do just that. These activities build community without forcing you to sacrifice teaching your subject. They also try to cover the various angles of community building.

The first section, **Set Your Expectations**, includes activities that set clear class expectations. By setting clear rules and communicating those rules to your students, you are helping the community persist. Activities in this section also help make clear that your classroom is a safe, respectful place to work hard and learn. Some of them are group-oriented ways to do needs evaluation. Others allow you to share class rules or good study habits in ways that also practice key teamwork skills such as listening to others, valuing others' contributions, sharing expertise to help the group, and finding compromise and resolution to conflict.

The activities in the **Working Together** section are the heart of

---

2   *See Google's Five Keys to a Successful Google Team: https://rework.withgoogle.com/blog/five-keys-to-a-successful-google-team/*

the book. These are 35 cooperative learning activities that get students working in teams on tasks and using language. Some allow students to practice teamwork skills. Some are primarily focused on language learning. Others focus on the theme of the class. And many are task-based team exercises that I find fun to teach and that students find fun to do.

I have included a section on **Getting-to-know-you Activities.** However, rather than being empty ice-breakers, these activities require group work and seek to help students feel a part of a larger community. Some of these activities will be familiar to readers of *50 Activities for the First Day of School*. I've included the ones that teachers and reviewers felt were particularly good at building classroom rapport. Others will be completely new.

There's also a section with five **Getting to Know Your Teacher Activities** that put the spotlight on you, the teacher. Of course, you can turn any getting-to-know-you activity into a get-to-know-the-teacher activity by modeling it for the class (and I hope you will do just that). However, these five activities are particularly well-suited to helping students get to know you. Don't forget that you are often a bit of a mystery and students are curious about their teacher as a human being. In an EFL class, you may be the only person from your country they've ever met. And putting yourself out there shows that you are a good sport and willing to build rapport with them.

Finally, please don't forget that building community and helping students work together isn't something that we do in the first week of class, and forget about. It's something to work at year-round by giving students multiple chances to work together, and continuously cultivating a classroom.

Resources

Many activities in the book involve a handout or a worksheet. Go online to http://www.alphabetpublishingbooks.com/resources-classroom-community-builders/ for free samples that you can download and print to use in your classroom, or adapt as you see fit. Sample worksheets are also included in this book after many activities.

Did something in this book go especially well? Did you come up with a variation or adaptation of something you found in this book? Or did something not go quite as you expected? Please share with other students. Join the **Classroom Community Builders Facebook Group** (https://www.facebook.com/groups/1861157320576399/) to post your success stories and your suggestions.

Set Your Expectations

Building community is about more than getting to know each other or even working together. It's also about having common expectations and ground rules. As a teacher, you want your classroom to be a studious and respectful space. This book begins with 11 activities that set a good tone and clear expectations in your classroom. The first two activities, Book Scan and Book Field Trip, allow students to grapple with the subject matter of the course. They can also work as needs evaluation activities, giving you an idea of your students' expectations and interests in the class, as well. Syllabus Scavenger Hunt and Classroom Rules Negotiation focus on class rules and policies. The remainder of activities introduce and help establish good classroom behavior, in fun student-centered activities that require group work skills.

Book Scan

This activity introduces students to the course and the textbook by taking a quick trip through the textbook. It works best early in the class, preferably on the first or whenever they first get their textbooks.

TIME	25 minutes
MATERIALS	The class textbook
LANGUAGE	Expressing preferences, "I like…", I don't like…", "I need help in…" Expressing expectations and wishes, "I hope that…", "I would like to…", Expressing interest, "I'm interested in…"

Procedure

1. Put students in pairs or small groups. Ask them to get out their textbooks.

2. Give them 5-10 minutes to look over the Table of Contents (or Scope and Sequence, if it's a language coursebook) and find one topic or unit that they both think is particularly interesting.

For academic subjects, ask students to discuss what they know about the topic and what kinds of debates or controversial issues are related to this topic. They can then talk about what more they want to know or hope to learn about it.

For language courses, have students to look over the topic or theme of the unit, and the language features to be taught. Ask them to discuss how well they think the topic and the language are matched in each particular unit. There are a few ways they can do this:

- Have them list some ways related to the theme they might use the grammar or vocabulary. Do they think it's a good match?

- Have them think of other situations in which they might find those grammar or vocabulary features useful. Could the author have chosen better language points for that theme?

3. Once they've discussed their impressions for 10-15 minutes in pairs, ask each pair to report back to the class one interesting statement or question they've come up with.

Book Field Trip

This activity is a more in-depth exploration of the book than Book Scan. Use a list of questions to guide your students through their textbook and let them get a sense of what they will be studying and what will be fun or challenging. This activity helps give students ownership of the class.

Time	20 minutes
Materials	*The class textbook, a list of questions about the textbook*
Language	*Expressing preferences: "I like...", I don't like...", "I need help in..." Expressing expectations and wishes: "I hope that...", "I would like to...", Expressing interest: "I'm interested in..."*

Procedure

Before class: prepare a list of questions that will direct students to some of the topics they'll be studying in the class. You can do this in a number of ways:

- Direct them to important chapter headings or diagrams. For example, you can ask, "What does the picture in chapter 2, page 23 show? What do you think that chapter is about?"

- Highlight important skills or key concepts with questions, such as "What will you learn about on page 42? Where might you use this kind of language?"

- Include some open questions that encourage them to explore the book on their own terms, such as, "Find a page that is particularly interesting to you.", "Find a reading that looks like it might be useful to you outside of class." Or have them find something in the book they already know and which their partner doesn't know. Ask them explain the concept or fact to their partner.

1. In class, hand out your questions and let them work on them in pairs.

2. To wrap up, let students share with the class and the teacher what they are excited to learn, what will be useful, what they think will be difficult, and what will be easier for them.

3. Be sure to address their concerns about the course and the topics. And of course, take notes on their answers to help you adapt the class to your students' interests and needs.

Variation

The activity is adaptable to almost any level. Lower level students can look at pictures or graphs, while more advanced students can read and engage with the text.

Syllabus Scavenger Hunt

This is an interactive way to go through the syllabus or student handbook. After giving students the syllabus, hand out questions and have students hunt for the answers.

TIME	*10-30 minutes, depending on the length of your syllabus.*
MATERIALS	*Copies of a syllabus or short handbook for each student, a worksheet with questions about the syllabus for each student.*
LANGUAGE	*Wh- Questions, classroom terms that may be on the syllabus such as final grade, exam, pop quiz, percentage.*

Procedure

Before class: Prepare a worksheet with either questions or cloze statements that students can answer from the syllabus or student handbook. Statements might include things like, "For what reasons can I get an excused absence from class?" or "The final exam is worth ___% of my grade."

1. Put students in pairs or small groups. Hand out the syllabus or rulebook and the worksheet.

2. Give students time to read the syllabus and fill in the worksheet, thus learning the rules for your class. The length of time required will depend on the length and elaborateness of your syllabus or rule book.

3. Go over the worksheet to be sure the students found the correct information and to address any questions or concerns.

Variations

- You can also give each group of students one question each to search for, instead of an entire worksheet. As you go over the answers, ask each group to give their answer, and then have the rest of the class confirm if the answer is correct or not.

- If you prefer giving a lecture at the beginning of class as a way of setting your expectations and informing them of the class rules, you can still make a handout as described above. In class, have students fill it out as you speak, so that students can use as a note-taking device. Since you provide the questions, you can be sure they will stay on track. And of course, making them take notes helps them internalize the information better than if they were simple listening.

Syllabus Scavenger Hunt

Search the syllabus and find the answers to the following questions. The answers to these questions contain the most important information in the syllabus.

1) What is the minimum grade to pass this class?

2) Fill out the chart of how your final grade is calculated below:

Participation _____ %

Homework _____ %

Essay _____ %

Final Exam _____ %

3) How many times can you be absent without it affecting your grade?

4) If you are absent _____ times, your participation grade will go to 0.

5) What should you do if you are absent?

6) How many essays will you write? How long will they be? When are they due?

Classroom Rules Negotiation

Research indicates, and my own experience concurs, that students are more likely to follow rules if they are a part of the decision-making process. In addition, getting them to suggest rules gives you an idea of what they think a classroom should look like, which helps you to understand their expectations for the class.

Time	15 minutes
Materials	*A list of myths and helpful facts about studying your subject.*
Language	*Classroom actions, classroom objects, modal verbs to express obligation,*

Procedure

1. Put students in pairs or small groups.
2. Have the group make a T-chart on a piece of paper. One column should be labeled *Should* and another should be labeled *Shouldn't*.
3. Tell each group to think of three behaviors for each side of the T-chart. That is, they must come up with three things they should do in the classroom and three things they shouldn't do.
4. Once they have done that, make a big T-chart on the board. Have each group write their rules on the board, skipping any rules that have already been written down. Alternatively, collect the rules and compile them yourself.
5. If there are a lot of rules or rules that seem unnecessary or inappropriate, you could start a class discussion on the reasoning behind each rule and then have a class vote on each rule, going down the list.
6. Write the final list of rules on a nice poster that you can display in class.

7. You can also have students vote on consequences. Ask them, "What should we do if someone…" completing the question with "talks on their cellphone?" or "doesn't do their homework?", for example. You should have some say here, but let students give some thought to what the appropriate consequences should be. This helps them think about why certain activities are not allowed and also makes them more accepting of the punishment.

What Does a Community Look Like?

This activity elicits what good teamwork skills are by having students imagine what a good classroom community looks like and feels like.

TIME	*10-15 minutes*
MATERIALS	*None*
LANGUAGE	*Comparatives, superlatives, personal information, numbers.*

Procedure

1. Write the word, "Classroom Community" on the board. Underneath it write, "What does it look like?", "What does it sound like?", and "How do we know we are doing it?". Leave some space under each question to write student suggestions.

2. Give students 3 minutes to think about the answers to each question. You may need to suggest some sample answers to help them understand what you are looking for. You can suggest an example such as, "A good classroom community looks like students having all the materials they need out on their desk before class begins. It sounds like one person talking a time. We know we are doing it, because everyone is free to speak up and share ideas and no one is excluded."

3. Have students share their answers with the class. You can also write some answers on the board in the appropriate spaces below each question.

4. Give students the chance to discuss the answers and which they feel are most important to having a good classroom community. They may do this in pairs or in class as a whole.

My Favorite Teacher

This icebreaker activity encourages students to reflect on what good and bad teachers do (and what they don't do). It also gives you an idea of their expectations, so you can be on their good teacher list.

Time	15 minutes
Materials	Paper and a pen.
Language	Past Simple to describe what other people did, action verbs

Procedure

1. Ask students to write "My Favorite Teacher" on a piece of paper. Underneath it, have them make two columns with the headings "Did" and "Didn't Do".

2. Give them a few minutes to think of their favorite teacher and why they liked them. Have them write two things that teacher did and two things that teacher didn't do. A phrase, or at most a sentence, is sufficient.

3. Now ask them to write "My Least Favorite Teacher" on the same paper. Underneath it, have them make two columns with the headings "Did" and "Didn't Do".

4. Give them a few minutes to think of their least favorite teacher and what that teacher did that made them their least favorite. Have them write two things that teacher did and two things that teacher didn't do.

5. Have them share some of the things they wrote, either as a class, or in small groups. Make sure they give a reason for their answer. For example, "Ms. DeCarlo always corrected our mistakes with a smile. We didn't feel embarrassed to make mistakes." Encourage the class to come to a consensus on what makes a good or bad teacher. Be sure to take notes and strive to be a good teacher!

Good Teacher / Good Student

Instead of comparing a good teacher to a bad teacher, you can also compare a good teacher to a good student. Often, it turns out both share similar qualities. I discovered this activity online a while back, posted by Emma Mendiola of San Antonio College.

Time	15 minutes
Materials	*A whiteboard or blackboard, or even a flip chart.*
Language	*adjectives to describe character, verbs to describe common classroom habits*

Procedure

1. Ask students to take 3 minutes to think about some good teachers in their past. These good teachers may include classroom teachers, or if students haven't had much formal classroom experience, any one who has ever taught them anything, including parents, or job trainers.

2. Divide the board in half. Write "Teacher" on one half of the board. Call on students to say what qualities a good teacher has, based on their reflection. As they speak, write their thoughts under the word "Teacher".

3. When the students have finished, ask them to take 3 minutes to think about what qualities a good student should have. Again, they can draw on classroom experience, or informal learning.

4. Write "Student" on the other half of the board. As before, have students list the qualities of a good student. As they speak, write those qualities on the board.

5. Now have students compare the two lists. Do they notice any qualities in common? You can highlight this by circling or underlining qualities that appear on both lists.

6. You can now ask students to think about what observable behavior matches with different qualities. For example, if students list "prepared" as a quality for a good teacher, ask what a prepared teacher does or looks like. One possible answer would be that a prepared teacher comes to class on time and has all the books and materials they need.

7. To finish, write out on a piece of poster paper the qualities that both lists share, or those the students agree are the most important for a good teacher and student. Hang it on the wall and tell students that you will strive to meet those qualities if they do as well.

Study Habit True and False

Polling the audience about common myths or misconceptions is a popular and engaging way to start a talk, so why not start your class that way? Give students a mix of true and false information about studying well and let them figure out which is which.

TIME	15 minutes
MATERIALS	*A list of myths and helpful facts about studying your subject.*
LANGUAGE	*Expressing opinions such as, "I think..." and, "I believe..."*

Procedure

Before class: think of some common myths about studying that you wish to dispel. Then think of some good advice about studying that you want your students to be aware of. Make a list of all the statements in which you mix up the advice and myths in random order. The balance of true to false is up to you, but aim for 5-7 items total.

1. Present the list to the class on the board, on a projector, or on a worksheet. Ask students to say which statements are true and which are false.

2. Reveal the answers and go over them with students, giving them an idea of best ways to study.

Variation

Instead of the teacher-centered approach of you producing language myths, have students come up with their own good and bad study advice to share with a partner or the class.

Language Learning Myths

Read each statement below. Then decide if you think the statement is True or False.

1. You have to see a word 10-15 times before you can recall it easily.	T / F
2. The best way to learn English is to never speak your native language.	T / F
3. If I work hard enough, I will can lose my accent in English.	T / F
4. It's more helpful to study a little bit every day than study for a long time 2-3 times a week.	T / F
5. The best way to learn to speak is to memorize vocabulary words and grammar rules.	T / F
6. When you learn something new, you may have difficulty with something you already learned, temporarily. Learning isn't always a straight line of progress.	T / F
7. Have a clear goal for studying language.	T / F
8. Try to learn only classical or formal English. Watching movies or listening to pop music will cause you to learn bad English.	T / F
9. You must be sure to correct every mistake you make.	T / F

Language Learning Myths Answer Key

1. You have to see a word 10-15 times before you can recall it easily. Learning words is a long process. You have to be able to recognize it, recall its meaning, and know how to use it yourself to truly learn a word. That takes a lot of repetition.	T
2. The best way to learn English is to never speak your native language. Using your native language to translate vocabulary or understand grammar can be helpful. Also, trying to speak English all day long for every need can be frustrating.	F
3. If I work hard enough, I will can lose my accent in English. At a certain age, probably before 12 years old, the way we speak is solidified in our brain. The good news is that accent has less to do with speaking clearly than prosody—your rhythm, intonation and inflection. And you can learn all of those.	F
4. It's more helpful to study a little bit every day than study for a long time 2-3 times a week. As with most things, practicing every day helps our brains remember better.	T
5. The best way to learn to speak is to memorize vocabulary words and grammar rules. While drilling and memorizing can be helpful, fluency comes from speaking without paying too much attention to grammar.	F

6. When you learn something new, you may have difficulty with something you already learned, temporarily. Progress is rarely straight. As you get better in one area, you may temporarily see setbacks in another area. However, your language level should be getting better.	T
7. Have a clear goal for studying language. Setting a clear goal helps you focus on what you want to learn. It also provides motivation to keep studying.	T
8. Try to learn only classical or formal English. Watching movies or listening to pop music will cause you to learn bad English. While you may need to learn standard formal English, you can still pick up vocabulary and grammar from many sources. And using English for something fun is very motivating, even if that fun thing is a pop song.	F
9. You must be sure to correct every mistake you make. Mistakes can fossilize but focusing on all your mistakes can be very demotivating and a waste of time and energy. Focus on important mistakes such as those that impede meaning or those that you make frequently or those that are important for the task you are doing at the time.	F

What Do You Know?

This is a way to find out what a class has already learned. Examples are given for lower level students as well as higher level classes.

Time	10 minutes
Materials	A whiteboard or blackboard
Language	Various

Procedure

1. Ask students to tell you one thing they know about English. Put some ideas on the board such as:

    I know that the word for _____ in English is _____

    If I want to do _____, I say _____.

    _____ is an informal way to say _____.

    _____ grammar tense is used to _____ .

2. Have students discuss their knowledge of English. This is a useful way to see what they know, what kinds of things they know, how they categorize knowledge, and maybe even dispel some myths.

Study Tip Share

Start off class by having students share their advice on how to study well. Good study habits is a nice topic to focus on at the beginning of class and letting students share their expertise makes for a positive environment.

TIME	15 minutes
MATERIALS	None necessary. Poster paper and markers optional
LANGUAGE	Classroom actions and classroom objects, adverbs of frequency

Procedure

1. Put students in pairs. Ask them to share one piece of advice for learning English with their partner.

2. Alternatively, have each pair agree on five pieces of advice. Then as a class you can whittle the list down to the top ten pieces of advice from all the pair.

3. Students can wrap up by writing their advice on posters to hang around the class. This provides some nice reminders for students throughout the course.

Variation

You can also give each pair a particular area of English. For example, ask pair A to talk about how to learn vocabulary. Have pair B talk about how to learn grammar, while pair C talks about how to practice speaking, and so on. Depending on time limits, you could then do a round of speed dating share, where students meet with each other for 1 or 2 minutes at a time and share their advice.

Good Classroom Habit Role Play

Getting students to act out good classroom habits keeps the focus on good behavior. Since our classrooms often seem to feature us telling students what they did wrong, they appreciate the chance to show off some of the things they do well.

TIME	20 minutes
MATERIALS	None
LANGUAGE	Modal verbs to express obligation, classroom actions and classroom objects

Procedure

1. Ask students to get into pairs or small groups and assign them an area, such as classroom behavior or studying for tests.

2. Then, ask them to think of one habit of a good student in that area and to make a short skit or role play demonstrating the habit and its benefits.

    These can be as general as, "Study every day" or as specific as, "Use flashcards to memorize vocabulary."

    You can also ask them to role play a model classroom, including a model teacher. They'll need some time to prepare for this, but it will let you also see what they think a good teacher looks like!

Working Together

The activities in this section are the heart of the book, activities that have students working in groups. Each of these activities should ideally require students to play a part in a team. That allows them to learn teamwork skills and understand the benefits of working together.

Different Thoughts

This activity helps students understand that there are multiple ways to approach a problem and that different members of their team bring different perspectives to a task.

Time	10-15 minute
Materials	A chair
Language	Commands, basic body parts

Procedure

1. Introduce the activity by putting a word that has multiple meanings and connotations on the board such as "rice" (which can be eaten in a lot of different kinds of meals), or "home" (which means different things to different people), or "true" (which means everything from honest to faithful to correct).

2. Ask students to say the first thing that comes to mind when they hear the word on the board. After getting a variety of diverse answers, emphasize that all the answers are correct and represent different ways of looking at the same thing.

3. Now put a chair in the front of the room. Put the students into groups. Tell them that they must come up with a unique way to sit on the chair. As they think of a new way, they can send someone up to demonstrate.

4. Keep track of the number of new, unique ways students think of to sit in the chair.

5. As the activity goes on, the question of what "sitting" means will inevitably come up. Groups may accuse each other of not doing it right. Be sure to encourage this line of thinking. What exactly does it mean to sit? Is kneeling a kind of sitting? Do you have to face the front? The idea here is to help students realize that there are different ways to think about things.

6. When students wind down, remind them that there are multiple ways to approach a task, meaning that there are multiple ways to solve tasks.

Variations

- You can set specific rules such as, "Feet must be off of the floor" or "Your bottom must be on the bottom of the chair"

- Have students come up with ways to fit their whole group on the chair, instead of just one person. You might need a spotter to make sure no one tips over and gets hurt.

- Ask students to think of different ways to use a chair (or another common object). For example, you can stand on a chair to reach something high. You can turn it over and hang things to dry on the legs. You can turn it on its side and make a hiding place or a shelter. Encourage creativity!

Sorting Line

While often used as a getting-to-know-you exercise, Sorting Line also works well as a teamwork activity. After all, students have to communicate information efficiently and organize themselves. And in some variations, students are not allowed to talk, meaning they have to come up with a way of communicating without words.

Time	5-10 minutes
Materials	None
Language	Comparatives, superlatives, personal information, numbers, dates.

Procedure

1. This activity works best in groups of 4-8 students so break your class into groups as needed.
2. Tell students that they must get into a line by height, with the tallest person on one side and the shortest on the other. Give them 2 minutes.
3. Check if they have done it correctly.
4. Now, tell students they must line up by birthday, with the people with early birthdays on the left and those with late birthdays on the right.
5. Once they have lined up, check that they are correct by getting everyone to tell you their birthdays.
6. You can continue by getting students to line up by alphabetical order of names, years studying English, years studying at your school or program, time in country, how often they take a shower, what time they wake up or got to bed, or any other quality that can be quantified and ordered.

Variations

- This activity can be made more interesting by not letting students talk. But in this case, do not expect perfect success.

- Another variation is to have the students choose the criterion and line up by it. You or the other students then have to guess the criteria.

In My Own Words

This activity works best in the ESL classroom or anywhere that your students speak different languages. And in fact, it isn't really an activity. It's more of a place where students can share their native languages with each other. It also creates an ongoing conversation between students, and increases their awareness of language at the same time.

Time	Varies
Materials	Poster board
Language	"Yes", "No", Thank you", "How are you?"

Procedure

Before class: put up a poster board on the wall and write a few common words or phrases in English, such as "Yes", "No", "Thank You", and "How are you?".

1. In class, show the poster to students. Tell them that this is a language sharing board and encourage them to write the same phrases in their own language. This is something they can do before class or during a break, but not during class itself.

2. Usually, the chart fills up within a week and a few wonderful things happen:

   Students start teaching each other their languages, which is a great bonding activity. Students who speak the same language will argue about how to translate words: "Bonjour doesn't mean 'Hi.' 'Hi' is too informal. I'll write 'Salut' instead."

   In the same vein, students will start thinking about how context, social status, and gender affect language. It's often these short common phrases such as greetings that are most dependent on context. Making students translate these phrases forces them to think about pragmatics.

Finally, you learn a lot of new languages. And if you start using some of those phrases in their native language, students will see that you view them as complex human beings with an identity and culture outside of the classroom. Outside my classroom, being able to say please, no, and thank you in different languages has come in useful from time to time.

How Do You Say?

Feel free to write how to say these phrases in your language.

Hello	Goodbye
How are you?	Thank you.
Please	You're welcome

I Am a Word

In this activity, each student holds a card with a word on it. They then have to arrange themselves to form correct sentences. This tests what students know about word order, verb tense, or parts of speech. It also gets them working together to rely on each other's knowledge of grammar and word order.

Time	15-20 minutes
Materials	Cards with words that make up a variety of sentences
Language	Sentence Structure and word order. Exact language depends on the target structure.

Procedure

Before class: choose a structure or grammar point you want to practice. Language features that work well with this activity include word order, verb tenses, gerund vs. infinitive, and prepositions-anything where students have to decide on the order of words and which words are included or not included.

Now, think of a sentence that uses that the target structure, and one that can easily take different words. For example, if you want to practice modal verbs, you could make a sentence such as "You should wear socks." It's easy to substitute other words for "You" and "socks" and also to rewrite the sentence with other modal verbs.

Write the words of the sentence on large cards or sheets of paper, one word per card, large enough to be seen from the whole classroom. Then add cards with other words that can be substituted into your sentence, For the modal verb example you could include other pronouns, other items of clothing, and of course other modal verbs.

Be sure to think of how changing the sentence might involve changing other words. For the modal verb example, you'll need a card for *to* because some modal verbs require the word *to*.

1. In class, put the cards on a table in front of the class.

2. Hand out the words of your original sentence to different students and have them form the sentence by standing in line in front of the class holding the cards.

3. Now ask a student to choose a new word and replace one of the students standing in line. For the modal example sentence, "You should wear socks.", you might have a student choose the word, "have" and replace the student holding the word "should". The sentence would now read "You have wear socks."

4. Ask students if the sentence is correct. Encourage someone to correct it, in this example by grabbing the card "to" and standing between Have and Wear.

5. Continue having students swap words in and out, checking if the sentence is correct or not. If it is incorrect, let students try to correct it. This might involve changing word order, adding other words, or taking out other words.

6. Continue until you feel you have a grasp on their understanding of the target language.

Sentence Auction

While sentence auctions are most often used as a review exercise, this activity can also be used to assess what students know about grammar or vocabulary. Students get a set of sentences, some correct and some not. They bid to try to buy the most correct sentences in this fast-paced, fun game.

TIME	20 minutes
MATERIALS	A set of sentences, some correct and some incorrect
LANGUAGE	Varies based on the target language

Procedure

Before class: Choose vocabulary words or a set of grammar points that you want to assess or practice. Write ten to twenty sentences that use the target language. At least half of them should be incorrect. A good strategy for creating incorrect sentences is to incorporate the most common errors students make.

You also may want to make pairs of sentences to guide students. For example, if one sentence is, "I enjoy skating.", another could be, "I enjoy to skate."

1. In class, put students into small teams.

2. Tell students that each team has $2,000 to use to buy sentences. They can bid in multiples of $50. Remind them that since they have a limited amount of money, they can only buy a limited number of sentences. Their job is to buy correct sentences only. Their final score will be the number of correct sentences they buy minus the number of incorrect sentences they buy.

3. Put the sentences on the board or hand them out in worksheets. Don't give them time to review the sentences.

4. Run the auction. Ask teams to bid on each sentence one at a

time, until there is a clear high bid. Keep track of who bought which sentence and also how much money the buyer has left. If a team runs out of money, it cannot bid anymore.

5. At the end, go over the sentences and reveal which are correct. Be sure to correct the incorrect sentences as a class.

6. Then add up each team's score by subtracting the number of incorrect sentences from the number of correct sentences they bought. The team with the highest score wins. If two team have the same score, the team with the most money left wins.

Cloze Paragraph

Cloze (or fill-in-the-blank) paragraphs are a simple way of creating an imbalance in information. Each student has information the other does not. Therefore they have to work together. It's also an activity that is highly customizable; You can turn any text into a cloze by blacking out words.

Time	10-15 minutes
Materials	*A passage in two versions, with different words or phrases replaced with blanks.*
Language	*Various question forms, various language depending on the target structure.*

Procedure

Before class: choose a cloze paragraph from the course book. If you are using your own reading then you need to make one copy of the text for every student in the class.

Prepare an A version and a B version by replacing different words or phrases with blanks in each version of the text. Preferably, the blanks should be staggered so that students alternate having missing information as they read the paragraph. You may want to chose random words or target particular language structures or parts of speech.

1. Put students in pairs. Give each partner the A or B version of the text. Make sure they do not show each other the text.

2. Tell students that each version is missing some information. Their partner has the missing information. In order to fill in the blanks, they need to ask their partner a well-formed question.

3. Have Student A begin to read the paragraph. When they come to a blank, they must ask Student B a question that correctly

asks for the missing information. Then Student A should write down the answer.

4. Next, Student B should read until they come to a blank. Now, Student B must ask Student A a question that correctly asks for the missing information and write down the answer.

5. When students have finished, they can compare their versions and make sure they got everything correct.

Variations

- If done as a way to preview a text, students could then go on to discuss the text as a whole.
- Have students guess what word is missing based on context clues before asking their partner.
- Rather than paragraphs, the cloze can be unrelated sentences.
- Turn it into a competition with prizes for the pair that finishes first.

Sample Cloze Master Text

This sample cloze focuses on comprehension of the text and asking basic Wh-questions. Thus names, things, and locations have been cut out of it. However, this exercise could focus on verb tenses, key plot details, or even pronouns.

Keep the original text for checking answers.

The original text

Secret Agent Jim Pond walked into the cafe. He looked for his fellow spy, Mr. U. U was sitting at a table near the back. He was wearing a red coat so Pond could recognize him. Pond sat down and asked, "Where is the target?"

"She's in her hotel room across the street."

"Good. And what is the job?"

"Your job is to watch and see who she meets."

"And who is she?"

"She is the thief who stole the Faith Diamond."

Version A

Fill in the blanks by asking your partner for the missing information. Then answer the questions that your partner asks you. Be sure to use well-formed questions. The blanks may be single words or longer phrases.

Secret Agent Jim Pond walked into the _____. He looked for his fellow spy, Mr. U. U was sitting at a table near _____. He was wearing a red coat so Pond could recognize him. Pond sat down and asked, "_____"

"She's in her hotel room across the street."

"Good. And what is the _____?"

"Your job is to watch and see who she meets."

"And who is she?"

"She is the thief who stole the Faith Diamond."

- -

Version B

Fill in the blanks by asking your partner for the missing information. Then answer the questions that your partner asks you. Be sure to use well-formed questions. The blanks may be single words or longer phrases.

_____ walked into the cafe. He looked for his fellow spy, _____. U was sitting at a table near the back. He was wearing a _____ so Pond could recognize him. Pond sat down and asked, "Where is the target?"

"She's in her hotel room _____."

"Good. And what is the job?"

"Your job is to watch and see who she meets."

"And who is she?"

"She is the thief who stole the _____."

Don't Say It

Many teacher have used this game to practice and review vocabulary in a fun way. In this game, students try to describe a word to their partner, but they can't use any of the most obvious key words.

TIME	5-15 minutes
MATERIALS	Cards with vocabulary words and words that are not allowed
LANGUAGE	Varies depending on the target words; Guessing phrases such as, "Is it a ...?", descriptive words and strategies, "It's not exactly...", "It looks a bit like a ...", "You use it when you...."

Procedure

Before class: make a set of cards with words you want students to practice with. Leave one side blank and on the other side, put the word, the definition and a list of words students cannot use. For example:

Racket
Definition: Used in tennis or badminton to hit a ball
Don't say: tennis, badminton, ball, Wilson, Head

---

1. Put students into pairs or small groups. Give each group a set of cards and make sure that the words are facing down so they can't see them.

2. Students take turns taking a card and describing the words to their partners, without saying the word or any of the key words in the definition. Student B must try to guess the word. This forces both students to think deeply about the definition of the word since Student A has to explain it and Student B has to guess

it. In the example of racket, Student A might say, "You use it to hit a ball, it's not a bat." Student A can also guide Student B based on their guesses.

3. When they are done with the card, students switch so Student B takes a new card and tries to get Student A to guess.

4. You can make this a competition to see how many words students can get right and which pair gets the most words right. In that case, pairs get one point for each word that is guessed correctly. They get zero points for every word that is not guessed or if one of the forbidden words is used.

Fill in the Picture

In this activity, students try to draw a picture or photograph from a description given by another student. Because students have unequal information, they need to work together. The content of the picture can be chosen to match the lesson or theme you are covering.

Time	10-20 minutes
Materials	One picture for every pair of students, in two copies, where each copy has only one half of the picture. The easiest way to do this is cut the picture in half and Xerox each half separately
Language	Prepositions of location, adverbs of location, visual adjectives, colors, directions; various nouns depending on the picture

Procedure

Before class: Find a picture you think your students would be able to describe. This can be done with any kind of picture or even a diagram or map. Make sure that the complexity of the picture matches the language skills of your students. Cut the picture in half and copy both halves in such a way that there is blank paper where the missing half is; students will be drawing the missing half of the picture.

1. In class, put students in pairs.

2. Hand each student a different half of the picture and ensure that they do not show it to their partner.

3. Have students take turns describing what is in their half of the picture so that the other student can draw it.

4. When students have finished, have them share their half of the picture and note how accurate their rendition is. Focus less on artistic ability and more on comprehension.

Variations
- You may want to give students some hints about the pictures, depending on their level and your theme. For example, you might tell them that they are all pictures of people or that they all have a tree in them somewhere.
- This can be done as whole class activity with students taking turns drawing on the board or on a large piece of paper.
- The student doing the describing can be allowed to correct the student drawing as he draws or not depending on communicative needs.
- Students can draw or select pictures themselves.
- Each pair can be given a portion of a larger mural that then has to be put together by the class as a whole.

Sample Fill in the Picture

Master Picture

Picture A

Picture B

Download and print out a full-size version of this resource at http://www. alphabetpublishingbooks.com/classroom-community-builder-activities

Picture Flashing

This activity is a great way to open a new theme or topic. Students are allowed to view a picture for a very short amount of time. They then have to describe or answer questions regarding the picture. As a group exercise, students will learn to appreciate each other's memory skills.

Time	10-20 minutes
Materials	An interesting picture or a picture related to the topic of the class
Language	Modal verbs of speculation, hedging language (I think, maybe, sort of), expressing an opinion; prepositions of location, adverbs of location, visual adjectives, colors; various nouns and adjectives depending on the picture

Procedure

Before class: find an interesting picture with lots of details, or one related to the theme of the class. Photos with people wearing unusual clothing or doing unusual things works very well.

1. In class, tell the students you are going to show them a picture very quickly. They should try to remember all the details they can.

2. Count down from 3. Then show the picture to the class for 15 seconds.

3. Put students in pairs or small groups to try to remember as much as they can about the picture. For lower level students, you can let them draw, as long as they are talking about what to draw as well so there is some language practice.

4. After a set time of 5 minutes or so, you can show the picture again for another 15 seconds.

5. After another 5 minutes, go over the picture as a class and see what details they remember.

6. You can extend this activity by finally showing students the picture and having them come up with a story to match it. Try any of these Collaborative Story Ideas or Reverse Story Picture.

Variations

- Start off by showing the picture to one student for a very short time, say 2 seconds. Ask that student to say what the picture shows. Then show it to a second student and ask them to say what the picture shows. Do this three or four times before showing it to the whole class. This piques interest in the picture.

- Another variation is to give students roles before showing the picture. Put students into groups and give each student something specific to look for. Student A might look at the background and setting, while Student B might focus on the foreground. Student C might focus on the main action. You could even ask students to focus on particular areas of the picture.

Sample Picture Flashing

Student Dictations

Having one student dictate to the other is a nice form of group work, ensuring each student has half the information needed to complete the task. Giving students the chance to provide input to each other is a nice bonus. These exercises work well for targeting a complex grammar structure as students are repeating larger chunks of text.

Time	*15 - 20 minutes*
Materials	*A set of sentences for students to read to each other, a version of the worksheet with only the even numbered sentences, and another version with only odd numbered sentences*
Language	*Clarifying questions such as, "How do you spell that?", "Can you please repeat that?" and "What did you say?"*

Procedure

Before class prepare a set of sentences with vocabulary or grammar that you want to target. Prepare a Master Copy with all the sentences. Prepare an A version with the even numbered sentences replaced by blanks. Prepare a B version with the odd-numbered sentences replaced by blanks.

- In class go over some language that students may need for the task such as, "How do you spell that?", "Can you please repeat that?", "What did you say?", "Did you say in or at?"

- Put students in pairs. Give each partner in the pair the A or B version of the sentences. Make sure they do not show each other the text.

- Instruct students to take turns reading their sentences to their partner. The student listening should write down the sentence verbatim so they will need to listen carefully. They will also probably need to use the questions that you went over at the beginning of the task, such as, "How do you spell that?"

- When both students are finished, they can swap papers and check their answers.

Variations

- Instead of sentences, you can give students questions to dictate to each other that they then have to answer or discuss together.

- Students can also dictate different genres of text including headlines, jokes or tongue twisters

- Students can create their own sentences given guidelines on what language feature to include. Just make sure that students are not going to be receiving sentences that they themselves wrote.

- After finishing, students can create their own sentences using the target form or function.

Sample Student Dictations

This dictation was designed to focus on a particular set of vocabulary words: *controversial, advertisement, enhance, consumer, purchase,* and *recycle..* You can design your own exercise to focus on other vocabulary or a language structure. Keep the Master Copy for checking answers.

Master Copy

1. It was a controversial decision that not everyone liked.

2. After seeing the advertisement in the magazine, I want to buy the new sports car.

3. We can enhance the helpfulness of our product by adding features that people really need.

4. A company must always serve its consumers first because companies make money from the people who buy their products or services.

5. I like these new smart watches, but I'm not sure I like them enough to actually purchase one.

6. I prefer to buy food that comes in packages you can recycle.

Version A

Read your sentences to your partner. Be sure to speak clearly and answer their questions. Then, listen as your partner reads their sentences to you. Write them down. Ask questions if you need help understanding.

1. It was a controversial decision that not everyone liked.

2. _____

3. We can enhance the helpfulness of our product by adding features that people really need.

4. _____

5. I like these new smart watches, but I'm not sure I like them enough to actually purchase one.

6. _____

- -

Version B

Read your sentences to your partner. Be sure to speak clearly and answer their questions. Then, listen as your partner reads their sentences to you. Write them down. Ask questions if you need help understanding.

1. _____

2. After seeing the advertisement in the magazine, I want to buy the new sports car.

3. _____

4. A company must always serve its consumers first because companies make money from the people who buy their products or services.

5. _____

6. I prefer to buy food that comes in packages you can recycle.

Twenty Questions

A simple, no-prep guessing game that is fun to play, requires a lot of descriptive vocabulary, and exercises critical thinking skills. Students learn to be detailed in asking questions, but they also learn to listen to each other, synthesize information, and use wrong guesses.

TIME	5-10 minutes
MATERIALS	None
LANGUAGE	Yes/No questions, various descriptive vocabulary depending on the target word

Procedure

1. Think of a thing. Preferably it should be a concrete object such as a book or a car, rather than a quality such as honesty. It could also be a job, a location, or a kind of person. You may want to choose an item in the room. You may prefer to choose an item from a theme or topic such as, "things you find in a hotel." In that case, tell students the category.

2. Have students guess what the thing is by taking turns asking questions. The rules are:

    - They can only ask Yes/No questions. So, they can ask, "Is it bigger than a book?" but they cannot ask, "How big is it?"
    - As a class, they can only ask 20 questions total. That means that they should listen to everyone's questions so they don't repeat a question and waste their time.
    - Students can take a guess at any time but a guess counts toward their 20 questions. This prevents students from just guessing instead of asking questions.

3. Let students ask their questions and keep track of the number of questions asked. Although you should answer only Yes or No,

you may want to help them out a bit with extra information as needed.

4. When the class has used up their 20 questions, give each student the chance to make one last guess. If no one has guessed correctly,

5. Follow up with a discussion of which questions were most helpful in guessing, and how multiple questions worked together to get useful information.

Extension Ideas

- You can model critical thinking skills by reverse-engineering questions. Now that students know what the object is, have them think about what kind of information would be useful for them to identify that object. What is unique about it? What sets it apart from other things like it: Size, use, where it is found, color, material? What questions could we ask to find out that information?

- You can extend this activity with a lesson about describing objects or using descriptive language.

Culture Shock

This simple activity uses culture as a ready-made source of content to help students meet other cultures and break down stereotypes. It also gives them a subtler understanding of culture.

Time	20-25 minutes
Materials	*A list of behaviors that are seen differently in different cultures or contexts*
Language	*Language to express an opinion such as "I think...", "In my opinion....", Hedging language such as, "usually", "in general", "I'm not sure but...." Verbs that describe common behaviors*

Procedure

Before class: Prepare a list of behaviors that may be interpreted differently in different cultures. It's good to have a mixture of positive or polite behaviors and negative or rude behaviors.

The list of behaviors can easily be designed to target a particular thematic unit such as behavior at a hotel or a particular set of vocabulary. It can include stereotypes for students to discuss or contain some of the most common differences between American culture and the students' home cultures.

While this activity works best in a diverse classroom, even students from similar backgrounds will often find regional, familial, generational, or personal differences.

1. Put students in small groups as mixed as possible by nationality, ethnicity, gender and age.

2. Ask them to discuss the behaviors and whether in their culture these behaviors are considered polite, rude, or perhaps neutral.

3. Encourage students to think about different contexts as well

as settings. Students can also consider regional, gender, and generational differences as well. For example, in the United States, gender and age play a huge role in how we greet people, whether we hug or shake hands for example.

Culture Shock Handout

Discuss the following behaviors with your group. Do you think they are polite or rude? Are there some times when they are more or less acceptable?

1. Giving up your seat to someone on the bus
2. Disagreeing with people older than you or in positions of power over you
3. Shaking hands with a stranger
4. Asking someone what their religion is
5. Ask someone what their ethnicity or nationality is
6. Kissing a friend on the cheek
7. Coming to work twenty minutes late
8. Telling guests that it is time to leave
9. Cutting in line
10. Holding the door for a woman
11. Giving money to homeless people
12. Allowing a work colleague to take credit for something you did
13. Paying for someone else's dinner at a restaurant

Jigsaw Reading

The jigsaw technique creates collaboration by giving each group of students a different part of a whole text. Because the students have different information, they must work together to understand the whole text.

TIME	*30-60 minutes*
MATERIALS	*A reading divided into different sections*
LANGUAGE	*Varies depending on the reading*

Procedure

Before class: prepare a reading by dividing it into equal sections. To ensure the sections are equal, consider not only length but also difficulty. A short paragraph with a lot of difficult language may be just as hard to read as long paragraph that tells a simple story.

1. In class, divide the students into groups. The number of groups should equal the number of sections of the reading.

2. Give each group one section of the reading. Each member of the group should have their own copy to take notes on. Allow students enough time to read their section.

3. Tell each group to take some time to discuss the reading. Each member must understand the reading thoroughly and be able to explain it.

4. When you think students are ready, put students in new groups. The new groups should be formed so that there is one student from each previous group. In other words, the new groups should have one student that has read each section of the reading.

5. In their new groups, students now explain their section of the reading in the order of the text. Make sure they make time to

take questions. You may also want to have them think about how the different sections of the text relate to each other.

6. When they are ready, separate the students and give them a quiz or test on the whole reading. You can also quiz the students orally on the sections of the text they did not read. For example, when you ask about section A, tell the students who read section A to be silent.

Extension

- Have students read the whole text and do other comprehension or vocabulary activities.

- Ask students to write three questions they have about other parts of the text and then read for the answers.

- Have students write the quiz questions for each other.

Variations

- The jigsaw technique can be done with listening texts as well, provided you have enough CDs and headphones or students can download the listening to their phones. Students would then listen to different sections instead of reading them in their initial groups.

- It can also be applied to a long assignment with students doing different parts of the worksheet and then teaching the other students.

- Do it online: Students can read their sections for homework and then record their thoughts on sites such as Voice Thread (https://voicethread.com) or Voki (http://www.voki.com).

PHOTOCOPIABLE

Sample Jigsaw Reading

This reading has been divided into four paragraphs of roughly equal length. The first paragraph and last one are the longest but also the simplest in vocab and context. Note that each section answers a clear question or has a clear topic and yet together they tell a whole story. Each student will learn from the others.

Here's a rough summary of each section to give you an idea of how I chose to divide them.

Section A is about Merrit and that he is happy.

Section B is about Bob's status and achievement, one reason Merrit is happy.

Section C is about Bob's promotion, a result of events in Section B and another reason Merrit is happy.

Section D is about more details of the raid from Section B, and focuses on Bob's thoughts after the promotion in Section C.

For the quiz, there are exactly two questions about each section so that no one student has an advantage. This quiz could be done in written form or orally, making sure that students who read that section are silent. Questions 9 and 10 talk about the reading as a whole and require synthesized knowledge.'

The Reading

A.   Merritt Hughes stood on the curb of the justice building watching his nephew until Bob turned the corner a block away. Anyone noticing the federal agent would have seen a slight smile of pleasure on his lips and he might have guessed that Merritt Hughes was greatly pleased by the events which had happened in the preceding hours.

B.   As a matter of fact, Bob Houston, a plain clerk in the archives division of the War Department, temporarily a provisional federal agent, had been the key figure in preventing an important theft.

C.   Through Bob's efforts a daring plot had been thwarted and the men responsible taken into custody. As a reward for this brilliant work, Bob had been made a full-fledged agent of the famous bureau of investigation of the Department of Justice.

D.   There were many thoughts in Bob's mind as he strode toward home that night. Only that afternoon he had led the raid on the east shore of Maryland which had resulted in the apprehension of the gang which had been attempting to steal the radio secrets. Then, after the return to Washington, had come eventful hours.

Excerpt from Agent Nine and the Jewel Mystery by Graham M. Dean (Public Domain)

Quiz Questions

1) What is the relationship between Merrit and Bob?

2) What mood is Merrit in?

3) What job did Bob do?

4) What is Bob's full name?

5) What is Bob's new job?

6) Did the criminals get away?

7) Where is Bob headed?

8) What did he do this morning?

9) Why did Bob get his promotion?

10) What crime did Bob stop?

Classroom Scavenger Hunt

A scavenger hunt is a fun and active orientation to the classroom. It's also a way to practice prepositions, location words, and classroom vocabulary. Students are given clues to follow to different places around the room or the whole building.

Time	5-10 minutes
Materials	*Scavenger Hunt Clues*
Language	*Comparatives, superlatives, personal information, numbers.*

Procedure

Before class: Prepare a series of clues, on small pieces of paper or index cards, that lead students around the classroom. The clues should lead to specific locations in the classroom. For lower-level students, these should be straightforward, such as "Look under the white bookcase." For higher-level students, they could be more complex, such as "Look under the tall furniture where we keep the things we like to read."

Choose one clue to be the starting clue. Place a second clue in the place the first clue indicates. Place a third clue in the place the second clue indicates, and so on.

Depending on how many students you have, you will want to prepare two or three scavenger hunts. You can do this by creating multiple copies of the same clues or by creating completely separate hunts. It is helpful to color code the clues by making one set all on blue paper and another all of yellow paper, for example.

1. In class, put students in pairs or small teams.
2. Give each team their first clue. The students should use that clue to find the second clue and then the third clue and so on.

3. You can reward students as they finish or make it a race and have a prize of some kind for the team that finishes first.

Variations

- You can also do a school-wide scavenger hunt. You will probably need to coordinate with other teachers and the school administration. This could make for an interesting way to do a school orientation, with teams being sent to different offices and classrooms to learn what is there.

- To make it more interesting, you can add an activity students must do before finding the next clue. For example, a clue could say, "Put a red book on the teacher's desk. Then find the next clue inside the dictionary."

- You can include a prize of some kind—a small candy or pencil or a fun certificate--in the place indicated by the last clue.

- Alternatively, you can make it a race with a prize only for the student who finishes first.

Simple Classroom Scavenger Hunt

Cut out each clue and hide them in the place indicated by the previous clue.

The first clue is under the bookcase.	The next clue is on the teacher's chair.
The next clue is on top of the cupboard at the back of the room.	The next clue is on the bulletin board.
The next clue is under the computer.	The next clue is taped to the board.
The next clue is on the windowsill.	The next clue is under the students' chair in the middle of the room.
The next clue is outside the door.	You did it!

Picture Words

Drawing pictures of words is a great way to practice vocabulary. This activity also gets students practicing communication skills by having one draw clues to a word, while the other one guesses the word.

TIME	*Varies*
MATERIALS	*A whiteboard, blackboard, or flipchart*
LANGUAGE	*Guessing, "Is it a ....?"; other vocabulary depends on the target words*

Procedure

1. Tell students you will draw a picture on the board and they have to guess what it is. Tell them that you cannot speak while they guess; you can only draw.

2. Encourage students to shout out answers as you draw. Be sure to respond to their suggestions. For example, if you are drawing a cow and they guess horse, add an udder or horns. For more advanced students, you may need to draw related words or little situations if the word is abstract. Alternatively, you can draw clues to the sound of the word: for "teaspoon" you could draw a teabag and then a spoon.

3. Students can also play the game in pairs or small groups. You may want to give them a specific list of words to choose from. Alternatively, you may want to limit them to a particular category or theme, such as "things you find at a hotel", or "adjectives to describe people's appearance".

Alibi

A fun lesson plan where students must come up with alibis as a group. They then get examined separately to see how well they remember their alibi and how detailed it was. This lesson works best with classes from 6 to 12 people. While theoretically it can be adjusted to students of any level, the Procedure is a bit confusing, so the activity requires strong group work and listening skills.

TIME	*45 minutes*
MATERIALS	*None*
LANGUAGE	*Wh- questions in the past, "Where were you?", "What did you do?"; crime-related vocabulary such as, "alibi", "suspect"; Past tense to tell a personal narrative*

Procedure

1. Tell students that a crime has been committed in your town. I like to make them silly so students don't get concerned. Include a limited time frame for when it was committed. For example:

   This afternoon, the mayor's office was stolen by a group of daring criminals. The mayor left for lunch at 12pm and the office was still there. Stan Johnson, a tourist, planned to visit it at 3pm but found it missing. Sometime between 12 and 3pm, the building was stolen.

2. Check that students know the words 'alibi' and 'suspect'. Then put students into groups of three students each and tell them that they were all together at the time of the crime. They must develop an alibi to explain where they were and what they were

doing. Explain that the alibi must be as detailed as possible because each member of the group will be examined individually and the group with the most mistakes or discrepancies is the guilty party

3. Give students 10-15 minutes (depending on their level) to come up with an alibi and rehearse all the details.

4. Once everyone is ready, have each group give a very brief summary of where they were, such as "at a restaurant", "in class", or "at home."

5. The other groups must write down three questions about that alibi to ask each member of the group. So, if a group says it was at the restaurant, the other groups might come up with questions such as, "What was the name of your waiter?" or "What did each of you have to eat?"

6. Pick one group to start and send all its members but one into the hall. The rest of the class (acting in the role of police investigators) will now ask their prepared questions to the group member still in the room. Make sure the class takes notes on the answers to the questions.

7. Once all the questions have been asked, bring the second member of the group in and ask the first member to step outside.

8. Have students ask the same questions, noting any discrepancies from the answers given by the first member of the group. So, if the alibi is eating at a restaurant and the first student says the waiter's name was Jim, while the second student says David, make sure that students make a note of that.

9. After asking all the questions of the second member, bring in the third member of the group. H

10. Once again, have students ask their questions and take note of any discrepancies from the first or second students' answers.

11. Once all the members of the first group have been interviewed, you can repeat the interrogations with the next group.

12. When everyone has been interviewed, the class should vote on which group is guilty based on how many discrepancies they found between answers by each member of each group.

Variations

- Only one group is named as suspects. The other groups are all police. This version goes quicker because each police group can interview a different suspect in a different corner of the room, all at the same time.

- Instead of letting students come up with the alibi, you can give them a general alibi such as "You were at the movies from 12-1, at a restaurant from 1-2, and at a coffee shop from 2 – 3. This makes it easier for lower-level students and it means the police can come up with their questions as the suspects are coming up with their alibis

- Instead of making the police remember all the details every suspect said and compare them, you can have police note down when a suspect says, "I don't know" or gets confused.

Follow the Directions

Successful group work occurs when the group has a clear, meaningful, and interesting task to accomplish. The goal of this community building activity is to get students to work together as a team and also to see how well they do following directions.

Time	20 minutes
Materials	Varies based on the projec
Language	Clarifying question such as, "What do the directions say?", "Can you repeat that?"; Wh-questions such as, "Where does this go?", and Which one goes here?

Procedure

Before class: find a simple project that can be done in class. You should make sure they have clear instructions and all the materials that they need. There are a number of sources of simple projects:

Build It (https://web.stanford.edu/class/ed284/csb/BuildIt/BuildIt.pdf) is an activity specifically designed for team building. Students are given simple directions on how to arrange colored bricks. The concept is easy to grasp so you can write your own directions if you prefer.

Origami is a great source of projects with easy instructions and simple materials i.e. paper. Here's a site with nice simple directions. (http://origami-amazing.blogspot.com.au)

Legos or other construction toys work well, too. Give students a specific project with instructions that they have to make or challenge them to build the tallest tower, or the longest bridge, for example. Frugal Fun (http://frugalfun4boys.com/2015/01/30/simple-projects-beginning-lego-builders) has a nice collection of simple Lego projects.

If you want to get messy, there are also great simple science projects (https://www.simplycircle.com/science-fair-projects-4th-grade) students can do, that often have fun results.

1. In class, put students into groups. Hand out any materials they will need for the project and the instructions for the task
2. Ask them to follow the directions in order to accomplish the project or task before them.
3. You can make the task a race where the team that finishes first gets a prize. You can also set a clear time limit. You can also pick a winner based on who does the project the best.

Variations

- You may want to have each member of the team take on a particular role to help teach students the various roles needed to accomplish tasks. Sample roles could include: the instruction reader, the double-checker, the supplies organizer and the alternative thinker (who comes up with new ideas).

- Make this a directions gap activity. Make sure each student contributes equally to the task by breaking up the directions so that each student has one part of the instructions. The easiest way to do this to literally cut the directions up into separate steps and distribute them evenly among the participants. Remind students that they cannot show each other their papers. They must talk together and help each other.

PHOTOCOPIABLE

Follow the Directions Sample Task

Cut out the shapes below. Then follow the directions to form a shape. When you think you have followed all the directions correctly and formed the correct shape, call your teacher over to check.

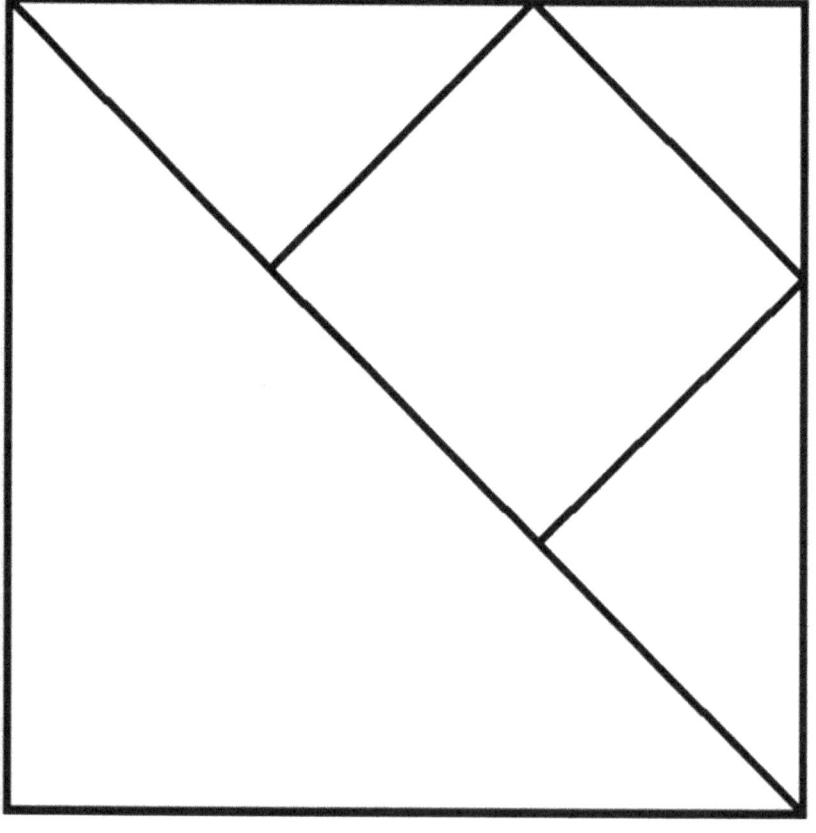

Directions

1. The square goes at the bottom. The edge of the square should be parallel to your desk or paper.

2. The largest triangle goes on top of the square.

3. All triangles should have their points facing up and their longest sides facing down.

4. The smallest triangle goes on top of everything.

5. The middle triangles go between the smallest triangle and the largest triangle.

6. No shape should overlap with another shape.

7. The triangles should all be centered with each other and the square.

Mystery Gap

I love doing short mysteries with my students. In this variation that guarantees students work together each, student has half of the clues. To solve the mystery, they have to share what they know.

Time	15-30 minutes
Materials	A short mystery and a set of clues cut into individual cards
Language	Modal verbs of speculation, hedging language (I think, maybe, sort of), expressing an opinion

Procedure

Before class: find a good short mystery. Some places to look include my book of Clue by Clue Games (http://www.prolinguaassociates.com/Clue%20by%20Clue/index.html) or Mystery Net's Get-a-Clue game, (http://www.mysterynet.com/get/) which posts a new free mystery every week. You could also adapt a short story mystery.

1. Put students in pairs. Give both students the initial situation or summary of the mystery. Let them discuss what may have happened.

2. Then give each of them half of the clues, alternating between the two students. Let each student try to figure out what may have happened, with the clues they have.

3. Finally let them share their theories, without sharing their clues. As each student speaks, the second student can correct them or give feedback based on the clues they have.

4. Finally, as a pair the students can try to solve the mystery. However, they should do so by discussing what they know based on the clues. Avoid letting students simple show each other their clues.

The Break-In Mystery

Somebody breaks into a store but takes nothing. Why?

The Situation

Tuesday morning, James Kilpatrick arrived at his clothing store to find the door wide open. However, when he checked the store inventory, he found nothing missing. Why did someone break into his store?

The Clues

1.   The owner of the store next door reported seeing a white van parked behind James' store Monday night.
2.   The day after the break-in, police got a phone call that James was selling pirated designer clothing in his store.
3.   The police found pirated clothing with fake designer labels on them hidden in a closet in James' store.
4.   James swore he was innocent, but he was fined $50,000. He couldn't pay and went out of business.
5.   Jacques' Fashion Boutique, which was almost bankrupt, reported much better sales after James' store closed.

Hints

Who benefited from James's store closing?

Could someone else have put those clothes in James' store?

The people didn't break in to steal anything. What did they do in the store?

The Solution

The High Fashion Department store framed James to put him out of business. They hired people to break into James' store. But the people who broke into the store didn't take anything. Instead they brought the fake clothing and hid it in the store. James didn't think to look for anything new in his store so he didn't notice. Then the owner of the High Fashion Store called the police and told them where to look for the illegal clothing.

Scenes from a Hat

This is a well-known improv acting game that encourages students to be creative by thinking of different ways to act out the same theme or topic. This activity is great for vocabulary review or role playing a situation. And improvisation helps build teamwork as students have to listen to each other carefully and work together to sustain the scene.

Time	*10-15 minutes*
Materials	*3-7 cards with situations on them that students can act out spontaneously*
Language	*Great for survival English and everyday situations*

Procedure

Before class: prepare a set of three to seven cards with situations on them that relate to class. These situations may be ones that students have recently learned about. Alternatively, they may be situations where students need to use a language function they have recently studied or you want to assess their use of. They should be relatively short situations that can be acted out in a few minutes, such as "Buying a Newspaper" or "Asking the Time"

1. In class, put students in groups. One at a time, read a card. Have the groups take turns acting out the situation. Emphasize that the goal is to improvise and speak naturally, so do not let students prepare too much and certainly do not let them write anything down to read.

2. After each group has acted out the situation, choose another card and have the groups act the new scene out. Be sure to have students act out new scenes in a different order, because the group that goes last will always have a bit of an advantage, having heard the other groups.

Variations

- Let groups go as many times as they can think of new ideas for scenes in the given situation

- Encourage students to make the scenes funny or unusual. They can make a funny character or think of strange ways the situation goes wrong.

- Hand each group slips of paper with a word or phrase on it that they must fit into the scene as they speak.

Difficult Situation

One source of discussion that generates a lot of student opinion is an advice letter. As students discuss the situation and debate their opinion of what to do, they gain appreciation for different points of view.

TIME	10-20 minutes
MATERIALS	A description of a difficult situation
LANGUAGE	Modal verbs to give advice and make suggestions; Expressing your opinion

Procedure

Before class: prepare a description of a dilemma that students can discuss and give advice about. A "Dear Abby" letter is a great way to do that. Make sure the situation is one students can understand and are likely to have differing opinions about.

1. In class, put students in groups. Hand out the letter. Have students read it, and find the most important facts. In the sample difficult situation handout, the key facts are: Steve is stealing food from the restaurant where he works; Steve is having a hard time because he is helping his father; Steve and Adam are friends and Adam doesn't want to hurt Steve; Stealing is very serious and Steve could get in a lot of trouble.

2. Give students 10 minutes to discuss the situation in their groups and try to agree on what advice to give Adam.

3. To wrap up, have each group tell the class what their advice is and why.

A Difficult Situation Letter

Read the letter below describing a problem. Then work with your group to first find all the facts of the problem. Finally, discuss what you think the writer should do.

Dear Problem-Solver

I have a problem. I work as a manager at a very nice restaurant. The other manager, Steve, is a really nice guy. We joke around at work a lot. And we even hang out a lot outside work. I also know that he's having s a hard time right now. His dad got sick last year. So now, Steve has to take care of him. Steve spends all his money on doctors' bills and medicine for his dad. On top of that Steve has two kids to take care of. His wife has an ok job, but it's still not enough.

The thing is, I think Steve has been stealing from the restaurant. I always see him going home with boxes of food. Look, we all take some leftovers home from time to time. And the chef sometimes makes us food to take home, like on the holidays or if he's making something really special. But Steve goes home every day with something in his bag. I asked him about and he acted really weird.

And it's not just meals. I saw him in the pantry the other day, pulling out bags of flour and sugar and putting them in a cardboard box. After work, I saw him putting that cardboard box in his car. So now he's stealing food supplies too. I don't want to lose him as a friend. And I know that he isn't stealing because he's greedy. He really needs the help to feed his family. But stealing is wrong. And he's stealing food now, but what if he starts stealing money? And he could get into a lot of trouble if he gets caught.

What should I do?

Befuddled in Food Service

Judgment

This is another activity to generate discussion and diverse opinions. Students have to judge what the punishment should be for people who have committed various social faux-pas, or other annoying behavior.

TIME	10-20 minutes
MATERIALS	A list of annoying behaviors
LANGUAGE	Modal verbs to make suggestions; expressing an opinion and giving reasons for it

Procedure

1. Write a list of annoying behavior on the board. It often makes sense to start with less serious behavior and move to more serious problems. Some examples that work well include:

staring	throwing litter on the street
singing in public	using bad words
talking to yourself	pushing people in a crowd
spitting on the street	cutting in line
	answering a cellphone at the movies

2. Put students in small groups to discuss what the punishment for these different behaviors should be. Emphasize that you are not looking for the actual legal consequences of these acts. Encourage students to be creative in thinking of how people should be punished (or why they don't deserve to be punished).

3. To wrap up, have each group share some of their best ideas with the class.

Collaborative Stories

Having students write a story together is a lot of fun. It demystifies the creative writing process. And it gets students talking about language together. The key is to make sure both students are equally involved in the process. Here are some ways to do it.

Pictures

1. Put students in groups and give them a series of pictures. You will need to choose if you want the pictures to be random or relate to each other.
2. Each student has to pick one or two pictures that they like.
3. The group then writes a story that makes a whole story using all the pictures that the students chose.

Vocabulary Words

1. Put students in pairs or groups and give them 3-5 vocabulary words. These should be words they know.
2. Give them a situation and have them write a story using both the situation and the words. For advanced students, make the situation completely unrelated to the vocabulary.

Storyboarding

1. Put students in pairs and give each student half of a storyboard, a set of pictures that describe a story.
2. Each student describes what happens in their storyboard to tell each other the full story.

As a variation, take a story board and cut it into thirds.

Give one student in each pair the first-third and give the other student the last third.

As a pair, they must figure out what the middle could be, coming up with a plausible series of events between the first third and the final third.

In the end, you can show them the missing bit and let them compare, or not.

Twist Ending

1. Have students write the beginning of a short story that ends in a twist or cliff-hanger. To help them with this, you can write some ideas for cliff-hangers on the board. Here are some easy to use ideas from Plot & Structure by James Scott Bell (https://www.amazon.com/gp/product/158297294X/)

   A sudden disaster: "At that moment, the car hit a tree."

   A sign or omen: "The dog dropped dead at that moment."

   A secret is revealed, "My mother said, "Actually I'm not your mother. In fact, I'm not even human!"

   A major decision, "I told my boss, 'I quit,' and walked out of the office without another word."

2. When the student gets to the cliff-hanger, they hand the paper to another student. Then each student reads the new story in front of them and continues it following the cliff-hanger.

3. In longer writing classes, you could continue this with a series of two or three cliff-hangers.

Questions First

This is another way to get students writing collaborative stories, but this is one is so unique, I couldn't resist separating it out. I adapted it from an idea by Mike Harrison.

1. Give your students a set of leading questions to a story that doesn't exist. This will take some creativity on your part. Good questions hint at a plot without being too detailed, such as, "Why did Anne go to store?", or "What did Bob see that made him drive away so fast he crashed his car?" The questions shouldn't be too random. Repeat character names, for example, and give some clear idea of events. However, leave room for student creativity.
2. Have students write answers to these questions individually.
3. Then put the students in pairs or groups. Each group must share their ideas and then together write a coherent story that answers all the questions.

Extension Ideas

- Students can swap stories and read for their favorite idea or scene. That can then be turned into a more coherent story.

- Have students swap stories and try to guess which parts came from different sources. Then discuss coherence and unity and have them talk about where they found incoherence and lack of unity.

Reverse Story Picture

This is a variation of Questions First where students generate questions of their own based on a picture you show them. There are a lot of levels of creativity required for this activity.

TIME	15-45 minutes
MATERIALS	An interesting picture
LANGUAGE	Varies depending on the story

Procedure

Before class: find an interesting picture that students can generate lots of questions about.

1. Show the picture to the students.
2. Ask students to come up with 3 questions they have about the picture. Encourage them to think about questions that could lead to a story. For the sample picture below, students might ask, "Where are these people?", "Why is she walking away from him?", "What do you think just happened?", and so on.
3. Put students in small groups. In groups have them share their questions, and choose the most interesting questions to answer.
4. Then have them work as a group to write a short story about the image.
5. Students can share their work and vote on their favorite story.

Sample Picture for Reverse Picture Telling

Plane Crash Survival

This fun activity gets students thinking about how different objects can be used in the context of surviving in the wilderness. It also forces them to have to rely on each other's knowledge. This version of this activity is adapted from an exercise on Scouting Web (http://www.scoutingweb.com).

Time	20-45 minutes
Materials	*Plane Crash Survival Worksheet*
Language	*Expressing opinions; hedging; agreeing and disagreeing.*

Procedure

1. Put the students in small groups. If you happen to know that some of your students are experienced outdoorsmen, break them up so that they are not all in the same group.

2. Hand out the worksheet and go over the situation: They are the survivors of a plane crash. They have a very limited number of items which they must rank in order of usefulness.

3. Give students some time to understand the situation and ask questions. Make sure they understand all the vocabulary. Try to emphasize that they have nothing else with them. This part may require a bit of creative story-telling on your part to explain why they don't have a cellphone or keys or something. As needed, tell them that cellphones fell out of their pockets, their luggage got smashed, and so on.

4. Once students feel they grasp the task, give them 15 minutes to rank the items on the list.

5. Then bring the class back together and have them share the items they think are most important. You can do this by going through the list item by item and having students vote with a

show of hands, who thinks it's important. Call on a few students to discuss why each item is useful or not useful.

Variation

To make the activity go faster, you can have them choose the five most important items, or choose three items they don't want to keep.

Plane Crash Survival Worksheet

You and your group were flying in a small airplane that crashed. None of you were hurt, but the pilot was killed. The airplane looks like it cannot be repaired. You are in the middle of the woods somewhere far from any towns or cities. You do not know exactly where you are. It is the middle of winter. It is very cold outside. There is snow on the ground and there is a running steam nearby.

You need to survive until the rescue team finds you.

You are wearing normal casual clothes for the winter, including winter coats. You go through the plane and find the items below. Everything else, including anything in your pockets, was destroyed or lost in the crash.

_____ A small ax

_____ A loaded gun

_____ Newspapers (one per person)

_____ Cigarette lighter (without fluid)

_____ Extra shirt and pants for each survivor

_____ 20 x 20 ft. piece of heavy-duty canvas

_____ A sectional air map made of plastic

_____ One quart of vodka

_____ A compass

_____ One big chocolate bar per person

Your task as a group is rank the items in order of importance for your survival. As you do so, think of the uses for each. You must come to agreement as a group.

Plane Crash Survival Notes on Each Item

Small Ax: Can be used to cut firewood, to defend against animals, to cut up animals for food, to dig a hole for a fire or for a toilet. Dangerous if someone gets out of control.

Gun: To defend against animals or to hunt for food, to start a fire, to make noise if they see a rescue team. Dangerous if someone gets out of control.

Newspapers: To read if you get bored, to help start a fire, to put inside clothes for warmth, to sit on to keep your clothes clean.

Cigarette Lighter: You may think it is useless without fluid, but it still makes a spark which can be caught by the newspaper, the string, or some kindling

Extra shirt and pants: Clothes to keep warm, fuel for a fire, material for a tent, maybe bright colors to signal a rescue team, something to sleep on.

Canvas: You can make a tent out of it. You can sit on it to keep off the cold snow. Could be used to make blankets.

Air map: To sit on, as the wall of a tent. Trying to locate where you are would be almost impossible since you don't know the exact route of the plane and the air map will only show things clearly visible from the air so small villages or buildings would be ignored.

Vodka: Good to start a fire. In small amounts to calm people down. Dangerous if people get drunk. Alcohol also lowers your body temperature.

Compass: Reflects the sun to create light. Again, you don't know where you are or where the nearest town so using it to try to walk somewhere is probably dangerous.

Chocolate Bar: Food. The wrappers could be used to help light a fire.

Mission to Mars

In this activity, students must choose which people to send into space in order to start a new civilization. Students must rely on each other's knowledge and opinions to complete the task.

Time	20-40 minutes
Materials	Mission to Mars worksheet
Language	Expressing an opinion; expressing agreement or disagreement

Procedure

1. Put students into pairs or small groups.

2. Hand out the Mission to Mars Worksheet. Have them read the situation. Make sure that they understand the situation and the task. Then have them look at the list of people and make sure that they know that jobs vocabulary. Note that every choice is meant to be difficult, above and beyond the fact that they have to limit themselves to five people out of eight.

3. Give the students 10 minutes to choose their five people.

4. You can then have the groups report back to the class, or go over each person on the list one by one, and have students discuss whether they chose that person and why or why not.

Mission to Mars Worksheet

The government has just discovered that in one month, a meteor will crash into the earth and destroy it. The government has one space ship that is ready to be launched. It can hold 5 people and fly them to Mars, where they will try to start a new civilization.

Your group has been appointed by the government to choose the 5 people who will be sent to Mars from the list of eight finalists. Remember that these are the people who will be responsible for starting a new human civilization.

The eight finalists are:

_____ A world famous 35-year-old male painter and sculptor.

_____ A 67-year-old male Catholic priest.

_____ A 23-year-old engineer and his 21-year-old wife, who never went to university. The engineer will not go without his wife.

_____ A 40-year-old policeman who will not go without his gun.

_____ A 32-year-old female sixth-grade teacher, who was recently arrested for stealing from her students.

_____ A 40-year-old female medical doctor

_____ A 25-year-old male author.

_____ A 1-year-old female baby

Discuss in your group and circle the five people you would put on the rocket to Mars. You must come to an agreement as a group.

Settlements

In this activity, students plan where to put a new settlement. In doing so, they must consider different geographical features and needs of their settlers.

Time	20-40 minutes
Materials	Blank map with various geographical features on it, such as the map of Newland
Language	Names of geographical features; expressing opinions; disagreeing and agreeing; modal verbs of speculation

Procedure

Before class, find or draw a map of an area with various geographical features, preferably without the names of existing towns.

1. Tell students that they are going to work in groups to find a place to make a new settlement.

2. Hand out the map you have prepared and give students time to go over it. Make sure students understand the different geographical features and any labels or legends. As needed, remind them that the place they choose should be able to meet all their survival needs: shelter, food, water, protection from wild animals, and links to the outside world. You can go over

3. Once they are ready, put students in small groups or pairs. Ask them to pick an area to settle in. Remind them that the whole group must agree. Give them 10 minutes to do so.

4. Then, let each group explain their choice to the whole class. You can allow some time for discussion of each group's choices as well.

PHOTOCOPIABLE

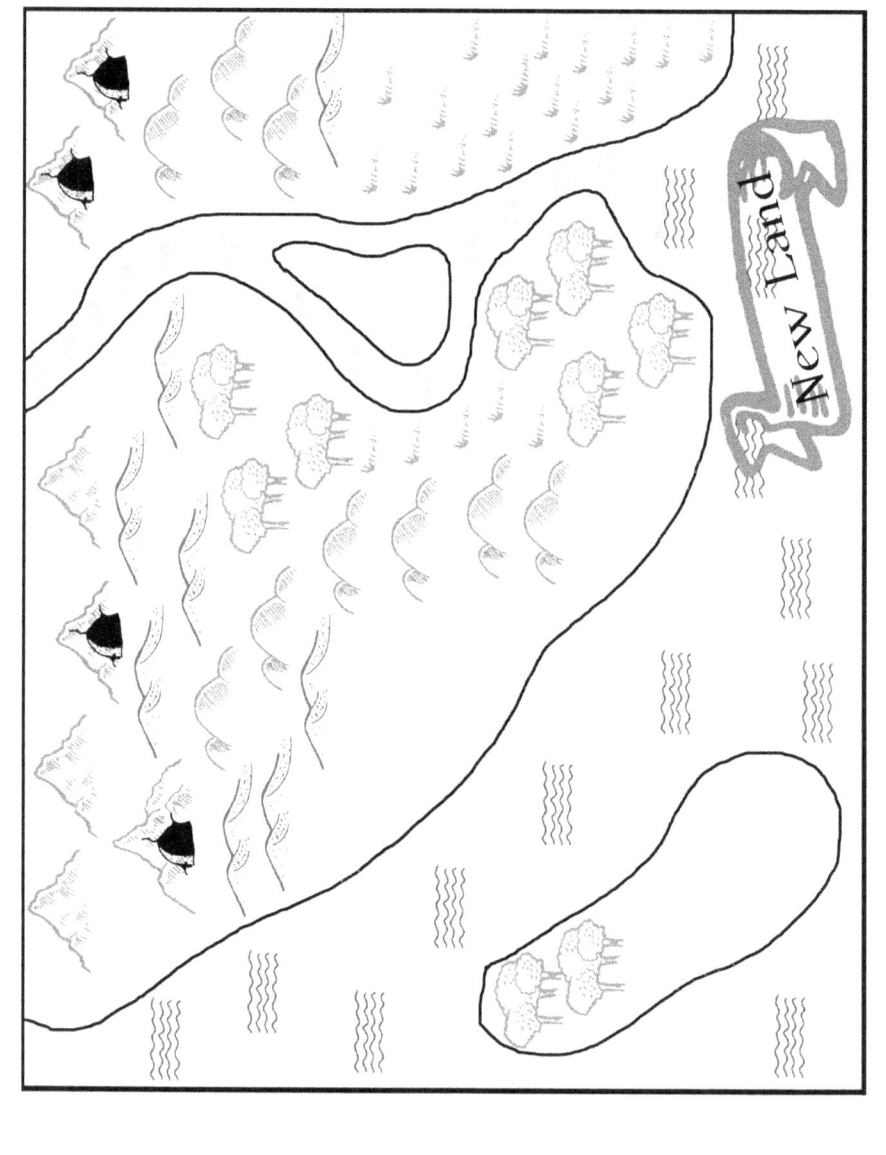

Create a New Country

In this activity, students come up with the rules for a new country or society including a map, a flag, and major laws. Students have to work together to agree on their country.

TIME	30-60 minute
MATERIALS	*Create a New Country* worksheet
LANGUAGE	*expressing opinions; disagreeing and agreeing; modal verbs of speculation; political terms such as names of forms of government, forms of economic systems, legal rights*

Procedure

1. Explain to the students that they have been charged with creating a new country. They can give their country any system of government they want, put it anywhere they want, and design both the geography and laws.

2. Put students in pairs or small groups and hand out the Create a New Country Worksheet. Quickly go over the worksheet to make sure they understand the terms and the kinds of answers that go on each blank. Make sure that they are familiar with the names of different forms of government.

3. The second page asks them to think about laws and character, including what the most important freedoms and rights will be, what kinds of economic activity there will be, immigration policy, what the holidays will be, and other laws. Encourage students to be as creative or as realistic as they like.

4. Give students 20 minutes to fill out the worksheet as a group.

5. After students have finished, let them present their country to the class or they can hang their worksheets on the walls and let other students browse them.

Constitution for a New Country

This document establishes the existence of a new country. The name of this country is: _____.

The language(s) spoken there are: _____
_____.

It is located _____
_____
_____

The official map of this country is to be drawn on the back of this paper, including symbols for the different geographical features.

The official flag of the country is as follows.

The population of the country is _____ people. It has a _____
type of government. The official religion (if any) is
_____.

The main laws are as follows:

1. Freedoms and Rights

PHOTOCOPIABLE

2. Economy

3. Immigration & Citizenship

4. Holidays

5. Other Important Laws

Debate

A debate, even a quick 20 minute one, gets students working with language in so many ways, and working together as team. Students in a debate are thinking critically, expressing opinions, hedging or qualifying statements, using transition words, rephrasing, and summarizing, all valuable language skills.

Time	*20-60 minutes*
Materials	*Pen and paper*
Language	*"Yes", "No", Thank you", "How are you?"*

Procedure

Before class: Choose a topic. For a quick debate without preparation, talking about their favorite teacher or favorite subject works well. They can also debate the best way to learn English or ways to prepare for a test. The topic needs to be something the class knows about and wants to talk about, so anything related to content covered in the class recently will work. It also needs to be something that is debatable, that has two or more sides to it. "The environment is important" is not a good debate topic because few people would disagree with it. "We should always stop business practices that can damage the environment because the environment is more important that any business," is more controversial and easier to debate both sides of.

1. Put students into two (or more) teams by position or opinion. You may want to assign positions or let students chose what team they want to be on.

2. Give each team 5-10 minutes to prepare a short opening statement, 3-5 minutes long, and decide who will deliver each speech.

3. Allow each team to deliver their opening statements without

interruptions. Encourage both sides to take notes and prepare rebuttals.

4. After the opening statements, alternate between both sides, asking students to raise their hands and address questions or comments to the other team. Continue this for a set period of time.

5. At the end, declare a winner based on who was more persuasive. You can consider how many reasons each team came up with for their side and also how well they answered the concerns of the other team.

6. As an extension, students can present their argument for a future class in the form of a poster or a slide show. If they are debating about a topic related to learning English, these posters can be valuable resources.

Variation

You can have a formal debate. In a formal debate the order of speakers traditionally is as follows:

Team A Opening Statement

Team B Opening Statement

Team A Rebuttal

Team B Rebuttal

(repeat Rebuttal speeches, if the teams are large)

Team A Closing Statement

Team B Closing Statement.

In a formal debate, the Opening Statements present the team's point of view and main reasons for that view. The Rebuttal speeches are mainly to answer the positions made by the opponents. They are general shorter. In the Closting Statements, each team repeats its most important ideas and reasons for them, which may include saying why they think the other team's logic was incorrect. You can find more detailed information about debates online.

Discussion Question

Rather than a full-fledged debate, students can simply discuss an important question related to the theme of the class.

TIME	10-30 minutes, depending on the discussion topic
MATERIALS	None
LANGUAGE	Expressing opinions, Hedging, Agreeing and Disagreeing

Procedure

1. Write a provocative question that you want students to discuss in class, or plan to provide an answer to during class. This class should be tied to the theme of the class or the work you plan to do in class. If it's the first day of class, it could be some fundamental issue related to the subject of the course.

2. Have students discuss the question in groups or as a class as a way of preparing for the class topic.

3. To use their answers later on, have students write down their answer and as many reasons as they can for their answer. This can be the precursor to a class discussion, debate, or even the beginning of pre-writing an essay.

Pyramid Discussion

This is one my favorite ways to do discussion in a large class. Because the discussion builds from small groups to larger, students get a lot of practice before having to speak before the whole class. Students also need to be sensitive to changing dynamics of the group. Most importantly this exercise teaches students to seek consensus.

TIME	10-30 minutes, depending on the discussion topic
MATERIALS	None
LANGUAGE	Expressing opinions, hedging, agreeing and disagreeing

Procedure

Before class: you may want to prepare a group chart. The class will be divided into pairs, then those pairs will form (ideally) groups of 4, those groups of 4 will form groups of 8, and then 16, until the class is whole. Unless you have 4, 8, or 16 students in your class, it's helpful to plan the thing out and figure out how to deal with odd numbers.

1. In class, give students the discussion question . Make sure students have all the language and resources that they need.

2. Put students into pairs and tell them to discuss the questions and come to an agreement.

3. Once students have agreed in their pairs, put the pairs together into groups of four.

4. In their groups of four, they should first report their conclusions and why and second come to an agreement as a group of four.

5. Once the groups of four have come to a conclusion, you can put them into groups of eight, where they will repeat the same Procedure: report their conclusion and then agree as a larger group.

6. Keep merging two groups until you get the whole class. You could then do a classroom debate or go over answers, or have a few people discuss their conclusions and why.

Role Play

Role plays can work very well with outgoing and creative students. Giving students a role can open them up. However, students at lower levels who don't have enough language to improvise in English may end up just reading their role card. So be sure to do role plays with students that are ready for it. In this example, students act out a press conference of a cosmetics company that makes defective products.

Time	20-60 minutes
Materials	A situation and role cards for each student
Language	Complaining; negotiating; agreeing and disagreeing

Note: There are role cards for 9 students. If you have fewer than 9 students in your class, hand out fewer roles, making sure there is an equal balance of people who work for Beauty, Inc. and people who do not. If you have more than 9 students, break the class into groups of 9, or add more roles keeping an even balance between pro-company and anti-company people.

Procedure

1. Hand out the Beauty, Inc. Situation and give students a few minutes to read it. Make sure they understand the situation.

2. Now hand each student one Beauty, Inc. Role Card and give them time to read it and understand it. I advise having weaker students prepare some key phrases they might want to use, or at least make some notes. Otherwise they will end up just reading from the card.

3. One activity to get students thinking is to have students write in one sentence who their character is. Then write what they want. Then write how they can get what they want in the situation. On the other hand, more advanced students will be able to get going pretty quickly.

4. Once you feel that students are comfortable with their roles and what they are going to say, tell them that the Press Assistant is in charge of the meeting and will decide who speaks. Often it's a good idea for you, the teacher to be the Press Assistant, but a stronger student can also handle the role. The Press Assistant should make sure everyone gets a chance to talk, and speakers can be prompted to stay on topic or respond to what has already been said.

5. You may also consider structuring the discussion. One structure is to give every person an opening statement and let the Press Assistant write a summary of their positions on the board to generate discussion later.

6. You might announce that the purpose of the meeting is to negotiate a compromise and the meeting will end when the company offers something that all of the victims can agree on. In this model, the journalists may play more the role of provocateurs.

7. Finally, another trick that works well in role plays and debates is to have each student repeat a summary of what the last student said before responding to it. This ensures that students listen and that they answer what people say instead of giving prepared speeches.

Variation

You can design your own role play surprisingly easily. The important thing is to have a conflict and various roles with diverse points of view. If you have a lot of students, or teach an advanced class, you can add subplots and drama.

It's good to choose issues that students can relate to, such as a family disagreement. You can also choose issues that students know a lot about. For an English for Oil Workers class I taught, we did a lot of role plays of business meetings, making budget decisions, analyzing environmental concerns, and choosing investment opportunities.

If you are lucky enough to be teaching a class with such a narrow focus, your students can help you write the role play by sharing the context they use English in, what the major issues are, and some of the more common sources of disagreement that come up.

Beauty, Inc. Role Play

The Situation

Beauty, Inc. is a large well-known company that sells beauty products to women. They have recently started a new line of products called "Success". The company wanted "Success" make-up and beauty products to have the image of being for rich and powerful women.

So they sent free samples to some of the most famous businesswomen and politicians. Unfortunately, there were a number of defects in the products:

- The blonde hair dye turned hair blue.

- The make-up caused allergic reactions in most of the women. Their faces are covered in rashes.

- The shampoo is so sticky that dirt and dust stick to it, making women's hair dirtier!

Beauty, Inc. is holding a press conference in order to try to explain these problems and control the damage to its reputation.

You will play one role at this press conference. Your task is to read the role card given to you by the teacher. The card will tell you who you are and what you want. Decide what kinds of things you will say to get what you want. Don't forget to talk as your character. Most importantly, have fun!

Role Cards

Company Spokesperson	Company President
Your job is to run the meeting. You can decide who speaks and who doesn't speak. You want to make the company look good. You also don't think these rich and powerful women should complain. They got the products for free! Try to be nicer to people who work for the company. Give them more time to speak, for example.	You are the President of Beauty, Inc. You knew about these problems before the products were sent out, but it would have been very expensive to fix them. You hoped the problem wouldn't be too bad. However, you do not want to admit this. You know that people are going to want money from you. Or to fire people. Try to give them as little as possible. Don't admit you did anything wrong.
Vice President	**Chief Scientist**
You feel bad about the people who suffered. You think the company should pay for medical treatment to fix the problems. You should probably fire some people too. You might need to pay some money. But you want to keep your job, of course! You didn't do anything wrong!	You told the President that the products needed more testing. But he ignored you and sent them anyway. You are worried that you will be blamed for these problems. You don't want to talk about why these problems happened. Let the company pay off the victims, but you want to keep your job and your reputation.

Mercedes	Secretary of State Blair Locke
You are a very wealthy businesswoman and popular lifestyle guide. You used the Success beauty products and your famous blond hair turned blue. You think you should be paid 1 million dollars for the problems you have suffered.	You are secretary of state and one of the most powerful women in Washington DC. Because of the Success products, your face is covered in rashes. You can't meet world leaders like that! You want the company to do a full investigation of what exactly happened. Anyone involved should be fired immediately.
Newspaper Journalist	Lauren
You are here to report on the situation. You are tired of big business hurting people. You want to ask a lot of tough questions to the company about whose fault it is and why.	You are a maid at a famous actress' house. She gave you her free Success beauty products. Now your hair is blue and very dirty and your face is full of rashes. You can't afford treatment. You think the company should pay to fix everyone's problems.

Cultural Role Play

This is an activity that that I adapted from the US Peace Corp's classroom guide, *Building Bridges*. I've seen similar activities done in intercultural competency workshops as well and my students always get a kick out of it. In this activity, students role play two different cultures and interact with each other. Then the class can discuss how cultural differences can be misinterpreted. If your class is from the same culture, you can frame the discussion in terms of individual personalities. As a teamwork activity, be sure to follow up by talking about how to resolve misunderstandings.

Time	40-60 minutes
Materials	Role handouts for two different cultures
Language	Small talk and social language, polite requests

Procedure

Before class: Clear some space in your classroom for students to mingle. Prepare role handouts for each group of students.

1. When the students come, divide them into two groups at random, Pollywhoops and Loopons. send them to opposite sides of the room. Explain that each group is from a different culture or society and that both groups are going to meet each other at an international students' party.

2. Give each group their own role sheet and give them 5-15 minutes to read and understand everything. They should also take this time to think about how they will act. Make sure that neither group can hear the other get ready though. It is worth spending time with each group to make sure that they understand what they are supposed to do and how their culture acts. If you have the time, you can practice with each group to make sure they understand the role cards.

3. Once the students are ready, tell them that they are at an international students' party and there are two different groups of students. Tell them to interact according to the rules of their cards. Give them a set time limit–20 minutes is usually enough and let them mingle. Only interfere if students break roles or you appear to have a real misunderstanding on your hands.

4. After the role play has finished, ask the Pollywhoops to guess what rules the Loopons follow and ask the Loopons what rules they think the Pollywhoops had to follow. Now ask them what they thought of each other. Did they find the other culture rude or interesting or polite?

Extension Ideas

- You can extend this by discussing how cultural misunderstandings can happen, by having students share personal anecdotes or stories they know about cultural misunderstanding, and the notion that no one's culture is the one and only true way to do things.

- Another direction for discussion is why learning about another culture before interacting with them is important. You can hand out both sets of rules from the role play and ask students to think about how they might have interacted differently had they known each other's cultural norms.

- Finally, you can talk about how culture is different from a role play. Is tradition really a set of strict rules you cannot help following? How do cultural norms vary over time, in different regions, and person to person?

Variations

- You can easily come up with your own role card to match the level of the students or perhaps to focus on particular vocab or concepts. Make sure that there is some conflict built in. Some habits of the Pollywhoops should be easily misinterpreted by the Loopons and vice versa. For example, Pollywhoops think the word "Hey" is a bad word. Loopons always begin conversations with the word, "hey". You may also want to change the names of the tribes to make sure you avoid any rude soundings names.

- Another variation to the task: Instead of just a party, you can give students some sort of task. For example, tell students that you all work for the same company and you must decide what to do about a scandal in the company. By giving students a concrete goal, they are less likely to just begin playing around. However, there is also the danger that they will forget their cultural role.

Cultural Role Play Cards

PollyWhoops

1. You prefer to talk to people from your own culture instead of others.

2. You only speak when spoken to. You do not like to start conversations with outsiders.

3. You don't like it when strangers get very close to you. If a stranger tries to get close to you, you move away. If they keep getting close, you may shout "Ho!"

4. If a stranger touches you, you will shout, "Ho" and turn your back to the person.

5. You like to have very short conversations. You do not like to talk for a long time. If someone tries to talk to you for a long time, you will walk away.

6. If you hear a member of your tribe say, "Ho" you will run over to help them. Push or pull anyone who is trying to touch another Pollywhoop or get too close.

PHOTOCOPIABLE

Cultural Role Play Cards

Loopons

1. You like to talk to new people from other cultures.

2. In your culture, touching someone on the shoulder or shaking hands is a sign of friendship. You do it a lot.

3. You like to talk to strangers and stand close to them so they understand you.

4. In your culture, you value small talk and being able to talk to people for a long time. You can talk about the weather, your clothes, food, a TV show you saw last night, anything, for a long time without stopping. You think being quiet is a sign of rudeness.

5. You don't like when people turn their back on you. You respond by tapping them on the shoulder until they turn around.

6. You do not like to be grabbed or pushed or pulled. If anyone tries to push you away, you will get upset and shout, "Woot!"

7. If you hear another Loopon say, "Woot!" you will run to surround them and protect them.

Getting to Know You Activities

Community starts with students getting to know each other. A good icebreaker or fun fact activity can create a more relaxed and friendly environment. Many teachers do these on the first day of class, but getting to know someone takes time, so it's worth spending a bit of class time on an icebreaker periodically. These activities also involve language use and of course team work skills

The first five activities are simple name games, because that's the first step to getting to know someone. And don't forget that it's not just about you learning their names. You want the students to learn each other's names too. I'm amazed how many classes I've had where two months in students are still calling each other, "that girl," and "the guy in the red shirt".

Name Tents

This is more of a teaching tip than an activity. Have students make name tents for their desks. Then encourage students to use each other's names until they have memorized them. It's a simple step, but one that pays off well and one that can be used for future activities.

Time	5 minutes (with extension activities 10-15 minutes)
Materials	A piece of notebook or copy paper
Language	Personal names

Procedure

1. Have students take out a piece of paper and fold it in half. Ask them to write their names on the bottom half and then fold them in half so that their name is facing out.

2. Ask students to stand the name tents on the front of their desk for the first week of class to help you memorize their names. Be sure to use your students' names every time you call on them to help you memorize their names.

Variations

- For beginner students, making a name tent can be a good introduction to writing and the alphabet.

- You can have students decorate the tags with their favorite colors or decorations if you like. Students can also add a fun fact about themselves or take their name tag with them when they start doing other Getting-to-know-you Activities.

- Some teachers use name tags as a jumping off point for various name game activities.

Going on a Picnic Easy Version

This is an old camping game that you can use to learn names. In the original version (see the next activity LINK), students have to guess the rule you are following. This adapted version helps you learn their names, first.

Time	10 minutes
Materials	None
Language	Personal names, "My name is....", "I'm bringing ....", common nouns

Procedure

1. Say, for example, "I'm going on a picnic. My name is Walton, and I'm bringing a watermelon." Choose an item that begins with the same letter as your name. Explain this rule to your students.

2. Call on a student to make a similar sentence about themselves. For example, the student could say, "My name is Ali and I'm bringing apples." If necessary, remind them that the item they are taking should begin with the same letter as their name.

3. When that student has answered, repeat your sentence and his. So you would say, "My name is Walton and I'm bringing a watermelon. His name is Ali and he's bringing apples."

4. Now call on a second student. The second student must make a sentence about themselves, such as "My name is Paula and I'm bringing plates."

5. Now ask the first student, Ali, to repeat his sentence and Paula's sentence. So he would say, "My name is Ali and I'm bringing apples. Her name is Paula and she's bringing plates."

6. Continue in this way with each new student introducing themselves and then the previous student introducing themselves

and the new student again. The repetition helps students to memorize each other's names.

7. If you are feeling brave, at the end, you can try to repeat everyone's name and item. This helps students feel that you were listening and that you care about learning their names.

Variations

- You can choose whether you want to limit them to items that would make sense to bring on a picnic. In fact, how useful the items the students say they are bringing makes for some great discussion and a good laugh.

- You can also choose another category of vocabulary that is more relevant to your class or that you want to review. This works for abstract sets of vocabulary, believe it or not. I've done it with adult business students as, "Going to Write a Business Memo" and we bring, "clear introductions," "bullet points", "greetings" and so on.

Going on a Picnic Guessing Game

This is the original version of Going on a Picnic and a fun way to practice student names. Note that you will need to know your students' names to play it, so don't try this on the first day of class unless you have students make Name Tents or even wear name tags.

Time	10 minutes
Materials	None
Language	Personal names, "My name is....", "I'm bringing ....", common nouns

Procedure

1. Say, "I'm going on a picnic and I'm bringing a...." Finish with the name of something that begins with the same letter as your name. Do not tell students this rule, however.

2. For example, I would say, "I'm going on a picnic and I'm bringing a watermelon." because my name begins with W.

3. Ask a student to tell what they will bring on the picnic. If the student correctly names something that begins with the same letter as their name, praise them and call on another student.

4. If the student does not follow the rule, say, "No, you can't bring that." This can get frustrating, so you may need to hint eventually that there is a rule about what they can bring. You can also give more examples for your own name. For me, it could be: a water bottle, a walking stick, waffles, or walnuts.

5. Another way to give a hint is to list some items that the student can bring with them, and see if they can figure out the common thread.

6. As each students figures out the rule, encourage them to chime in and also help the other students until everyone gets it. You

can then do this as a chain activity with everyone in the class saying everyone's name and what they will bring.

Variation

You can choose whether you want to limit them to items that would make sense to bring on a picnic. In fact, how useful the items the students say they are bringing can be a great source of discussion and a good laugh.

Toss a Ball

This name-learning game adds some action, making it a little more dynamic and memorable than other activities to memorize names.

Time	10 minutes
Materials	None
Language	Personal names

Procedure

Warning: Be sure to use a ball that is not too hard, as not all students are good at throwing or catching. I'd recommend a soft squishy ball or a bean bag of some kind.

1. Throw a ball gently to a student to catch. Ask the student to say their name.
2. Prompt that student to throw the ball to another student. When that student catches it, ask that student to say their name.
3. Continue in this way with students throwing the ball to one another and the student who catches the ball saying their name.
4. Make sure that the ball is always thrown to a new student, so that everyone catches the ball and says their name once.
5. After a few rounds, introduce a new rule. Now, students must announce the name of the student they are throwing the ball to. If they accidentally throw the ball to the wrong student, they get a strike. If they get three strikes, they have to sit down fr the rest of the game.

Variations

- Students can catch the ball and name the student who threw it, as well as their own name. This can even be done as a mini-dialogue: "Thanks Sarah. I'm Mei."

- You can have students throw the ball to the same students in the same order every round or have them throw the ball at random.
- When you start having students announce whom they are throwing to, you can introduce a second (or third or fourth) ball, so students are constantly having to listen for their name.

Fun Fact Memory Chain

This is a fun game that gets students learning about each other. More importantly, there's lots of repetition of names. This game works best for classes of 5-15 students. If your class has more than 15 students, this activity will take too long.

Time	10-20 minutes, depending on the size of the class
Materials	None
Language	Personal names, "My name is....", present simple first person and third person to tell facts about yourself and others, "I have...", "I am...", "He has...", "She is..." Past simple.

Procedure

Before class: make one card for every student in your class and put a number on each card, starting from one

1. Find the student with the number 1 and ask them to say their name and one interesting fact about themselves. Try to nip in the bud any facts that could apply to most your students to prevent a lot of repetition, which is boring and counterproductive.

2. Now find student 2. Student 2 has to introduce student 1 by repeating their name and their fact and then say their own name and a fact about themselves.

3. Student 3 must repeat student 1 and student 2's introductions and then introduce themselves in the same fashion.

4. Continue in this way until all the students have gone. Then tell the students that it's only fair that you repeat all of them. This is a great way to remember names and also to show that you are listening and care about them.

    If a speaker forgets a name or fact about a student, get the other student to repeat their name or fact to the forgetting student. Then make the forgetting student repeat it. The more repetition, the better everyone will remember everyone's names.

Where Are You From?

This activity works well with students from different countries or different parts of the country. It also creates a resource you can use many times, a map of where students are from.

Time	10-15 minutes
Materials	A map of the world or a regional map
Language	Wh- questions, names of countries, languages

Procedure

1. Hand out sticky notes or similar labels to students. If your map is on a bulletin board, you can use small strips of paper that students can pin to the map.

2. Tell students to write down their name on the paper and stick it to the map on the place they are from.

3. Have the students look at where their classmates are from and form one question they have for a fellow classmate. This should be based on where they are from and might include asking about their language, culture, or food.

4. Students then find the person they have a question for and ask it. Allow them to chat for a few minutes.

5. Students then report to the class one interesting thing they have learned.

Same and Different

This is a simple interview activity where student find things they have in common and differences as well.

TIME	10 minutes
MATERIALS	None
LANGUAGE	Present simple first person and third person to tell facts about yourself and others such as, "I have...", "I am...", "He has...", "She is..."; Yes/No questions such as, "Do you like...?", "Do you have", Wh-questions such as, "What's your favorite...?", Where have you been..?" Comparative structures such as, "We both like...", "Neither of us likes...".

Procedure

1. Put students in pairs and have them question one another until they find two similarities and two differences.

2. Have them report back on the most interesting similarity or difference.

3. Students can also create a Venn Diagram, with two circles that overlap in the middle. They record the similarities in the overlapping area and differences in the outer areas.

Variation

Have the pairs find five things they have in common. Then put two of the pairs together to form a group of four. Have the group of four find five things in common among the four of them. These may or may not overlap with the similarities they found in pairs.

Now combine the four into groups of eight and have all eight students find five things in common or as many as they can. Keep going, forming bigger groups until you have the whole class together again

Identity Circles

A quick activity that demonstrates how we construct our identity and how we relate to different groups. Like the Same and Different, students are encouraged to find things they have in common as well as differences.

Time	10 minutes
Materials	a pen and paper
Language	Present Simple to talk about themselves, their jobs, and hobbies, such as "I am a...", "I like to..."; names of groups; relationship words; Comparative structures such as, "We are both ..."

Procedure

1. Have students think for a few minutes about five labels that they think apply to them. You can make suggestions to help them such as father, mother, student, good friend, gardener, stamp collector, or intellectual. The goal is to have them come up with five ways they identify or think of themselves.

2. Ask them to write the most important label on a piece of paper and circle it.

3. Now have them write the second most important one on a piece of paper and make a larger circle around that word and the first circle, so they end up with two concentric circles.

4. Then ask them to write the third label and yet another concentric circle. Continue in this way until students have five concentric circles and five labels.

5. They can then share their papers with the whole class or in a small group. Encourage students to look for similarities and differences.

Me Bag

While many people do Me Bags in primary school, the activity can easily be adapted to be more complex. I first heard did this activity in graduate school.

Time	10 minutes
Materials	three objects that students will bring to class
Language	Names of objects; present simple to talk about themselves, such as, "I like...", "I often do..."; Names of hobbies, occupations, and family relationships

Procedure

Before class: ask students to assemble three objects and bring them to class in a bag. This is a great one to model, so consider bringing in objects of your own and introducing your objects on the day you assign this task.

1. When students come in with their bags, have them introduce each item one at a time with the class or in a small group. Allow some time for questions before moving on to the next student.
2. There a wide range of criteria you can give for the objects. I've included some suggestions below. You can choose three different criteria or ask students to bring in three objects from one category.

    An object that is important to them or tells something about themselves.

    An object that relates to their interest in learning English

    An object that represents their family

    An object that represents their friends

A favorite food

A favorite book

Something they use every day

An object that represents a hobby

An object that represents their job

An object from their country.

Something that shows how they belong to a particular group, such as an ethnicity or a professional group.

3-2-1 Introduction

A simple getting-to-know-you activity that I learned about from Shelly Terrell. It feels very familiar, but can be adapted in so many ways

Time	5-10 minutes
Materials	Pen and paper; 3-2-1 worksheet is optional
Language	Present simple to talk about themselves; modal verbs to talk about hypothetical situations; names of hobbies and occupations

Procedure

1. Ask students to take out a piece of paper and write three interesting facts about themselves, two hobbies, and one dream job.

2. Ask them to find a partner, swap information, and then report one interesting thing about their partner back to the class.

3. Alternatively, you can hang the papers on the wall, have students find an interesting one, and then form a question to ask the person who wrote it.

Variation

This activity can easily be adapted by picking completely different topics for students to share such as:

ways to study

favorite sports

hobbies

secret skills

favorite foods

favorite bands

things you did over vacation

favorite place or places in the world

presents you've received

things you would never do for a million dollars

favorite person or people

reasons for studying this subject

something you would be doing now if you weren't in class.

3-2-1 Introduction Worksheet

YOUR NAME

Write down 3 interesting facts about you
2 things you like to do for fun
1 thing you'd be doing now if you weren't in class.

3 Things About You
1
2

2 Hobbies
1

1 Thing You'd Be Doing Now

Never Have I Ever, Classroom Edition

This is an adaptation of a well-known party game in the United States. It's probably so popular because it happens to be a great way to learn interesting facts about people and start conversations.

Time	5-10 minutes
Materials	None
Language	*Present perfect to talk about things they have done in their lives, such as, "I've been...", I've never been..."*

Procedure

1. Tell your students to think something that they believe many people in the class have done but that they have never done themselves. Some common examples might include flying on a plane, speaking a particular language, eating a particular food, or going to a particular place.

2. Have one student start by sharing their idea, beginning with "Never have I ever..." So Student A would say, "Never have I ever flown in an airplane." For lower-level students you can have them say, "I have never..." All the students who have done the action should now raise their hands.

3. If only one student raises their hand, that student should be encouraged to tell the whole story of how and when they did that thing. In the example of an airplane ride, they can tell the class where they went and why and what they thought about flying.

4. Keep going around the room until everyone has said their statement or every student has raised their hand.

Variations

- Instead of doing this in front of the whole class, students can mingle and ask each other, "Have you ever...?" plus their idea. If they find a student who says "Yes", they should ask for details. Students can then report back to the class something interesting they learned about a classmate.

- Have students think of something they have done, but no one else in the room has ever done. They can then mingle, asking each other, "Have you ever..." plus their idea. Every time they find someone who has done the action, they have to share details and then think of a new action. Students can then report back something interesting they have learned about a classmate.

Who Wrote That?

Students mingle in this activity that involves matching an interesting fact to the person who wrote it.

Time	15 minutes
Materials	One strip of paper for each student big enough for students to write a sentences on
Language	Present simple to tell facts about yourself, "I have...", "I am..."; past simple and present Perfect to talk about experiences in the past

Procedure

1. Hand out one slip of paper to each student. Ask students to write an interesting fact about themselves on their paper, preferably something that no one else in the room knows.

2. Collect the papers and mix them up. Give each student one of the slips of paper. If the student gets their own paper, have them give it back and give them a new one.

3. Each student must now find the person who wrote the slip of paper in their hands by asking questions of each other. Do not allow students to show each other their papers. You can also ask them to lead up to the subject naturally. For example, if their paper says, "I love cooking,", they cannot ask, "Do you love cooking?" Instead, they can ask leading questions such as, "What are your hobbies?", or, "Do you enjoy spending time in the kitchen?"

4. When they find the person, they can engage them in conversation and learn more detail about the interesting fact.

5. You can wrap up by asking each student to say one thing they learned about someone else in the class.

Class Averages

Students survey each other to learn about their classmates and find out the average age, height, and other information about the class. Gets students mingling and it's a great introduction to graphing and calculating.

TIME	Varies
MATERIALS	Pen and paper
LANGUAGE	Yes or no questions; Wh- questions; personal information such as name, grade-level, age; numbers

Procedure

Before class: think of a list of information you could find out about your students, or ask them to make their own list. Examples of information might include height, grade-level, age, years studying English, number of languages spoken, number of jobs held, or family size. You can do qualitative information such as favorite food or favorite movie, but unless there's overlap, students won't come up with an average (or most common) answer.

1. Put students in pairs or small groups to interview the class and find out this information about each student. Alternatively, each pair or group can choose to collect different information. So Group A finds out about height and age while Group B asks about years studying English, and number of languages spoken and Group C asks about something else.

2. Once students have collected the data, they should figure out the average (or most common) value for the class.

3. You can then discuss which information was most similar and which was most different.

Class Survey

In most getting-to-know-you activities, the student chooses what they want to say about themselves, or the teacher tells the students what to ask. In this activity, the students decide what they want to know.

TIME	*10 minutes*
MATERIALS	*None necessary, pen and paper are optional to make a written questionnaire*
LANGUAGE	*Wh- questions*

Procedure

1. Ask students to think of something that they want to know about their classmates. This should be a survey-style question such as "What is your favorite food?" or "What languages can you speak?"

2. Have the students form a question and then go around the room asking their question to the other students in the class. Depending on your goals, you could also have students write a questionnaire with or without answer choices.

3. Once students have asked everyone in the class their question, they can compile the results and report to the class. For example, "Hamburgers are the most popular food in the class; 50% of the class like them; 20% of students say their favorite food is sandwiches; and only one person likes chicken nuggets." You can adapt your expectations to the level of your class.

Group Profile

This is a way to have students get to know each other, to build a sense of community, and practice language. I adapted this activity from one I found in Tessa Woodward's book, *Planning Lessons and Courses*.

Time	*10 minutes*
Materials	*None necessary, optional pen and paper to make an official questionnaire*
Language	*Wh- questions; Yes/No questions; Quantifiers such as, "Most of us", "Some of us", "Half of the class"*

Procedure

1. Ask the class a survey type question such as, "How many of you live our class?", or "How many of you like chocolate?" Have students raise their hands to answer.

2. Record the number of Yes answers on the board and make a sentence about the result, such, "Most of us live near the school" or "No one likes chocolate." You can also have students form these results.

3. Continue asking questions and forming statements about the class.

4. To wrap up, you can have students say something interesting they learned about the class. Encourage them to look for patterns or correlations.

Variations

- You can also shift to questions about English study, or what students expect to get out of the class. In this way, this activity can become a form of needs evaluation.

- You can have students ask questions. Students can also begin doing some statistical analysis of the class practicing the language of percentages and correlations.

4-3-2 Fluency Intro

The 4-3-2 fluency activity, which I first discovered in Scott Thornbury's book, *Uncovering Grammar*, helps students speak more fluently as they repeat a story in shorter and shorter time periods. The repetition and time pressure also helps students be less reserved. I've applied it here to a getting to know you activity.

Time	20-25 minutes
Materials	None
Language	*Present simple first person and third person, to tell facts about yourself and others, "I have...", "I am...", "He has...", "She is..." Past simple to talk about past experiences*

Procedure

1. Designate half of your students as As and half as Bs. An easy way to do this is to go around the class pointing to each student and alternating between calling them A and B.

2. Put them into pairs with one A and one B.

3. Tell the class that the As will start the activity by talking about themselves for 4 minutes. You can give them a minute to collect their thoughts, but do not let them write anything down. If you feel students need it, you can give them some suggestions for things to talk about, such as their hobbies, families, or their interest in the class.

4. Count down from three and then let them talk. Be sure to time students and stop them at 4 minutes. It can be challenging to talk about yourself for four minutes, but encourage them to keep going.

5. Now put them in new pairs of A and B. Tell the As that they will talk about themselves again, going over the same information

they told the previous student. This time, however, they only have 3 minutes to do it. Tell them to focus not on talking faster, but on speaking more fluently and also on focusing on important details. Of course, they are welcome to add new content or qualifying things they said before.

6. Again count down from three and time the students, having them talk for exactly 3 minutes.

7. Put them in new pairs of A and B one more time to talk about themselves.. This time give the As 2 minutes. This should result in fluent speaking and concise introductions.

8. Once the As are done, repeat the activity with different partners. This time have the Bs do the talking.

9. This works well if you have the As stand in one line and the Bs in another line, standing facing each other. At the end of each talk, students can step to their right to face a new partner.

10. The basic activity, giving a speech for a certain amount of time and then having less and less time to do it in, works wonderfully to improve fluency and help students express important points. Research even indicates that this activity helps students focus on grammar because they don't have to think as much about content on the third repetition. And it can be used in a variety of settings. It even works as a writing exercise where students can move from 3 paragraphs to 2 to 1, for example.

Snowball Fight

This variation of Who Wrote That is extremely popular with students because they get to throw things around the classroom.

Time	15-20 minutes
Materials	One piece of white copy paper per student
Language	Present simple first person and third person to tell facts about yourself and others, "I have...", "I am...", "He has...", "She is..." Past simple, Present Perfect to talk about experiences in the past

Procedure

1. Hand out a piece of white copy paper to each student.

2. Have each student write one interesting sentence about themselves on the paper. Then have them crumple up their paper into a ball.

3. Tell students that you will count down from three. At three, the students should throw their paper ball to a random place in the class. Try to discourage them from throwing them as hard as they can at a friend.

4. Count down from three, and let them throw their papers. If you want to let them have their fun, you can have them pick up a snowball near them and throw it again. I recommend a maximum of three throws before getting back to work.

5. After throwing, have each student finds a snowball near them. They should open the snowball, reads the sentence, and try to find the person who wrote it by asking questions of each other.

6. As in Who Wrote That, you can make this harder by telling students that they cannot ask questions that directly address the fact in the paper. They must approach the topic indirectly.

Snowball "Texting"

Take Snowball Fight to the next level, by having students carry out a conversation with each other. Students will be pleased as they still get to throw things around the classroom.

TIME	20-25 minutes
MATERIALS	One piece of white copy paper per student
LANGUAGE	Language present simple first person and third person to tell facts about yourself and others, "I have…", "I am…", "He has…", "She is…" Past simple, Present Perfect to talk about experiences in the past

Procedure

1. Hand out a piece of white copy paper to each student. Have each student write one question that they would like to know about a classmate on the paper. When they are finished writing, have them crumple up their paper into a ball.

2. Count to three and then tell the students to throw their papers around the classroom at random. You do not want them to be able to keep track of who has whose paper. Try to discourage them from throwing them to their friends. You can let them throw the papers up to 3 times, or just once.

3. After throwing, have each student find a snowball near them, open it, and read the question. They should then write an appropriate response to the question.

4. When everyone is finished writing, tell the students to once again crumple the paper up again and then throw it at the count of three.

5. After throwing their papers, they should once again find a snowball near them, open it, read the conversation and add a

response. Make sure students are continuing the conversation and not simple writing non-sequiturs on the paper.

6. Continue in this way until you feel students are satisfied or set a time limit.

Get to Know Your Teacher

Of course, students also want to get to know you, the teacher. When I was teaching English in a school in Kazakhstan, the first day was full of students interrupting to ask if I liked basketball and what my favorite kind of car was. I quickly learned to include a getting-to-know-the-teacher activity in my lesson plans for the first day of class.

First Day Letter

Write your students a letter and ask them to respond as a way of getting to know them. To modernize the lesson, make it an email or a blog post.

Time	10 minutes to write a letter, 20 minutes for students to read and respond to the letters
Materials	A letter to your students, pen and paper for each student
Language	Present simple to tell facts about yourself, Past simple to talk about yourself in the past; future tense to talk about expectations

Procedure

Before class, write your students a letter. Include some personal information about yourself that you think your students want to know about you (And that you are willing to tell them). You can talk about your family, your hobbies and what you have been doing recently. You may also want to talk about why you became a teacher or something you love about your subject.

You should definitely include information about the class, such as what kinds of things you will be doing and what your expectations are for the class. This is a subtle way to generate interest in the class.

Be sure to include questions for the students in the letter such as, "What are your hobbies?" or, "What are you looking forward to in class?" The goal is to make it easy for students to answer your letter.

1. If you have contact information for your students, you can send the letter in advance. Otherwise in class, hand out the letter to each student and let them read it.
2. Then have them each write a response to you. You may want to

do this in class or assign it for homework. Depending on the class, you may want to teach letter format or even do a mini-lesson on register and tone for personal letters.

3. Collect the letters and read them. Use them to learn about your students, their interests, and their motivations for taking the class.

4. You can follow up by telling the class the most interesting thing you learned about each one of them or by writing them short notes of acknowledgment, such as, "Interesting that you want to be a doctor!"

Variations

- If you have access to student addresses or emails before school begins, you can send them your letter before school and ask them to write back or bring their answer to class.

- You can also reimagine this lesson as an email or blog post. In fact, if you have a class blog or web page, you could write an actual post online and have them leave their answers in the comment section or as new blog posts.

Ask the Teacher

This activity plays on the curiosity students often have about their teacher. It's also simple, no-prep, and provides good practice in asking basic questions.

Time	5-10 minutes
Materials	None
Language	Yes/No and Wh- Questions

Procedure

1. Draw a big question mark on the board.

2. Tell students that they can ask you anything that they want. If you are teaching beginners, this is a good chance to assess their use of questions.

3. You may also want to focus on cultural appropriateness of questions if students ask you questions that are generally considered rude to ask a stranger in English-speaking countries.

4. Let students ask for as long as you think appropriate. 5 to 7 minutes is usually enough.

5. You can follow up by asking the students to answer the questions that they have asked you. If you make this the rule from the beginning, you will cut down on rude questions quickly.

Tell Me about Me

This is basically a variation on Ask the Teacher . It's another way to satisfy students' curiosity about their teacher. This activity works best when you have students who have had you before, possibly in different classes. However, it is not for the weak of heart. Students can be rather undiplomatic in their assessments.

Time	10 minutes
Materials	None
Language	Present simple second person to tell facts about someone else, Past simple second person to talk about someone in the past, Expressing opinions and hedging language such as "I think…", "Maybe…", "You could be …"

Procedure

1. Draw a big question mark on the board.

2. Tell students that you are going to begin by asking students to say what they know about you. This might be from your appearance or what they have heard or what they think is true of teachers. Allow 5-7 minutes for this.

3. One at a time, let students guess things about you, correcting them when they are wrong. As necessary you can draw students' attention to things such as the presence or absence of a wedding ring, your clothes, or things you might have placed on the desk. You can also ask leading questions such as, "Do you think I am well organized or not?", and draw their attention to the way you have arranged your papers.

4. In a small class with brave students, you can ask students to volunteer to stand up and let the class talk about what they know about that student.

Correct the Teacher

This is a fun way to introduce yourself that also tests your students' note-taking abilities and memories.

Time	5 minutes
Materials	A short prepared speech about yourself
Language	Language to express opinions and hedge such as "I think…", "Maybe…", "That must be true because…"

Procedure

1. Prepare a short speech about yourself. One or two minutes is sufficient. You might want to include information about your qualifications, your hobbies, your current life or anything you think students should know or want to know.

2. Tell students that you are going to talk a little bit about yourself. Ask them to take notes as you speak because they will have to recall some details.

3. Now, tell students you are going to tell them five things about yourself. Four will be true and one will be a lie. The lie will contradict something that you have already told them. In other words, they should be able to detect the lie based on the short speech you just gave them. Ideally the facts should also relate to the speech you gave them, as well. If you told them you used to live in Ghana in your speech, you might tell them now that you were in the Peace Corps, for example.

4. Let students refer to their notes or consult with each other to try to find the lie.

5. Now you can have students play the same game, writing a short speech about themselves and then presenting five closely-related statements, one of which is untrue.

Answers on the Board

Put some information about yourself up on the board and have students try to make you say those words by asking you questions. It's a great getting to know you activity that also practices questions and answers.

Time	15 minutes
Materials	A whiteboard or blackboard, or even a flipchart pad
Language	Wh- Questions

Procedure

Before class: think of a few basic questions about yourself that have simple answers. It's best to come up with a few typical small-talk questions like, "Where are you from?" or What is your favorite sport?" and a few less typical questions like, "When did you finish college?" or "What kind of car do you have?"

For more advanced students, you may want to include more advanced questions such as, "What do you love about being a teacher?" or "What job would you want to do if you weren't a teacher?" It is sometimes possible to target a particular grammar structure, but it's not easy since there's often more than one way to ask the same question.

1. On the board write answers to the questions that you have thought of. Do not write the questions themselves however.

2. Tell the students that it is their job to make you say the answers that are on the board. They should do this by asking you questions they think the answers will match.

3. As students ask questions, answer them honestly. If they get close, you may want to give them a hint. For example, if you've written 1999, the date you graduated from university on the board and a student asks, "When did you finish high school?"

you could say something like "I finished high school in 1994, and I went to university after that." Depending on the level, decide how strict you will be about their question forms.

4. Once students have guessed all your answers, they can play the game with partners, putting their answers on a piece of paper instead of a board.

Tips for Building Community

These are some general tips and tricks for getting through that first day. Please feel free to add your own advice, tips, tricks or first day hacks in the comments!

1. Be sincere and consistent. This applies to disciplining bad behavior, talking about yourself, and the way you convey yourself in the classroom. A teacher who shuts down a conversation about a TV show because it's not relevant to the class, but lets another student go one about a shared favorite band, will be seen as playing favorites.

2. Be particularly strict about any shows of disrespect to other students. It may seem obvious, but if you want your classroom to be a safe place, there should be zero tolerance for teasing or insults. This includes not only making fun of people's backgrounds or clothes, but also mocking them for making mistakes. If students don't feel safe making mistakes in your class, they won't experiment and learn.

3. Remember, icebreakers like Memory Chain have students revealing facts about themselves. Make sure no one is being made fun of for something they revealed to the class. You may want to quickly go over what kinds of topics people usually bring up in icebreaker activities. For example, romantic status is not usually a comfortable topic, nor is religious or political affiliation.

4. On the other side of the spectrum, students may produce facts about themselves that are not particularly interesting. That defeats the point of an icebreaker. I can't tell you how many students I've had that say where they are from as their interesting fact about themselves.

    In a class that's 70% Saudi and 25% Chinese, for example, national origin is not a particularly personal or unique fact. So, model what you mean by an interesting fact. That means, if you are doing lots of classroom community builders (and you should be), you'll probably want to have a lot of interesting facts about yourself, ready-to-go off the top of your head. Be sure that they don't just parrot your one answer by giving them a few examples.

Considerations for Grouping Students

Sometimes you will be putting your students into random groups and there are a number of ways to do that. My favorite ways, often the simplest, include having student count off or having them form a group based on where they are sitting in the classroom.

However, sometimes you will want to more carefully engineer your groups. In team-building exercises, it's useful to put together groups with different skill sets. For discussion exercises, it's nice to include a diverse range of backgrounds and personalities. And in other cases, you need teams that share a particular characteristic. I've found that sometimes putting the quiet students in one group can increase participation, for example. I'll even admit to sometimes putting friends together in a group, on purpose, despite every instinct in my body because groups that get along well can often work together well.

Unfortunately, I can't predict what your needs for your activity or project will be and I don't know your students or classroom as well as you do. I can't tell you how to put together the perfect group for activity. I can, however, provide a list of things to take into consideration when building groups.

Gender: Men and women often have different opinions on the same topic. However, in some cases, men in a mixed gender group may try to dominate the discussion and the task. On the other hand, in some cases, a group of all men may spend more time deciding who the leader is than getting the work done.

Language: If the group shares the same L1 or another language besides English, they can rely on that language to communicate. If the group has different L1s, then they will be forced to speak in English. Both are desirable for different tasks. One danger to look out for is groups that are unbalanced. For example, if you have four Spanish speakers and one Arabic speaker in a group, the Spanish speakers may revert to Spanish quite a bit, leaving the Arabic speaker on their own.

Cultural Background: Groups that come from the same cultural background are likely to approach tasks in similar ways. Diverse groups are likely to come to the table with diverse approaches. There are advantages to both dynamics, of course. In a discussion, it's often useful to have students with different backgrounds and assumptions about the world and values. It's more likely that they will disagree and be forced to express and defend their opinions.

On the other hand, drawing too much attention to the social group of the participants can detract from cooperative learning. A key teamwork skill is learning to treat your fellow students as individual people, not a member of a social category. Of course, economic, racial, and social identity are real factors in your classroom and can play an important role. So, when selecting groups with diverse social, ethnic, and economic backgrounds try not to draw the students' attention to that.

Language Competence: In some cases, your students may have different levels of language ability. You may teach a mixed level class. You may be doing a class session that is open to the whole school or even the public. Even if your class is supposed to be at the same level, they may have different competences in the language needed for this activity. If group students by level, the more advanced groups will probably finish first or need more complexity to the task. Groups of mixed levels can lead to students helping each other, but students may get frustrated working with each other, as well.

Quiet vs. Loud: As every teacher knows, one loud student can dominate a discussion over 4 quiet students. On the other hand, a quiet student can explode if they are unable to get a word in edgewise for a long time. So there needs to be a balancing act. Sometimes, a group of all loud students and a group of all quiet students ends up being more interactive than a heterogeneous group.

Leader vs. Follower: Similarly, a student who likes to take the lead can take over a group quickly. Now, this can actually bring out the best in students who prefer to follow. That might seem counter-intuitive but some students don't feel interacting in a vacuum. They like to have someone take charge. It actually opens them up. In fact, I've found it's the leader-types who can shut down if they are not in charge. A group of all leaders can end up being a group of the winner surrounded by sullen losers who do nothing!

These are some factors to consider. As I said above, you know your students best and you know what you want to accomplish. I can only provide you some things to think about. Don't be afraid to experiment and figure out what exactly works best for your class

About the Author

Walton Burns is a teacher and materials writer from Connecticut. He fell in love with teaching English in the Peace Corps in Vanuatu in 2001. He was teaching Francophone Melanesian students in Vanuatu so they could complete high school equivalency degrees and become the first in their families to study in university. They were truly inspiring.

Since the, he has worked around the world teaching a diverse range of students from Russian oil executives who needed to improve their English for business, to Kazakh scholarship recipients off to study in foreign universities, to Afghani high school students on the an exchange program, to middle-schoolers in an extra-curricular speaking class.

He began his writing career in 2007, selling lesson plans on his blog. As demand grew, he began seeking out professional gigs, mostly helping fellow teachers develop lessons for their classes and developing lessons and assessments for the school he was working in.

After winning a few lesson plan contests, he came to the attention of the Nick Robinson Agency and was very successful there. He continues to work with Nick and ELTJam, as well as independently.

Walton publishes his own books and lesson plans, writes and edits for publishers, and designs activities and lesson plans for language schools. Some of his clients have included Oxford University Press, Macmillan, Pearson, Compass Publishing, 2LTI Testing and New Horizons Language Schools.

Since 2014, he has been part of the leadership team of the Materials Writing Interest Section of the TESOL Association, the international association for English language professionals.

Picture Credits

Cover Illustration Cienpiesnf/Adobe Stock

page 47, Fill in the Picture: Clkr-Free-Vector-Images/Pixabay.com. CC0 (Public Domain)

page 50, Picture Flash Illustration: Cormoran/The Project Gutenberg ebook, *English Fairy Tales*, by Flora Annie Steel, Illustrated by Arthur Rackham.

page 88, Reverse Story Picture: Petunyia/Adobe Stock

Free printable and downloadable worksheets at:

http://www.alphabetpublishingbooks.com/resources-classroom-community-builders/

∼

Join the

Classroom Community Builders Facebook Group

https://www.facebook.com/groups/1861157320576399

Share your success stories!

www.ingramcontent.com/pod-product-compliance
Lightning Source LLC
Chambersburg PA
CBHW070618300426
44113CB00010B/1572